THREE RINGS

THREE RINGS

A TALE OF EXILE, NARRATIVE, AND FATE

DANIEL MENDELSOHN

UNIVERSITY OF VIRGINIA PRESS

Charlottesville and London

Page-Barbour Lectures for 2019

University of Virginia Press
© 2020 by Daniel Mendelsohn

First published 2020

ISBN 978-0-8139-4466-1 (cloth)
ISBN 978-0-8139-4467-8 (ebook)

1 3 5 7 9 8 6 4 2

Library of Congress Cataloging-in-Publication Data is available
for this title.

Cover art: Page from Greek edition of Homer's *The Odyssey* (*Omerou Illias* = *Homeri Illias*, vol. 2 [Venice: Aldus, 1504]). (Special Collections Research Center, University of Chicago Library)

For Glen Bowersock and Christopher Jones

CONTENTS

THREE RINGS

I

The Lycée Français

Il valente uomo, che parimente tutti gli amava, né sapeva esso medesimo eleggere a qual più tosto lasciar lo dovesse, pensò, avendolo a ciascun promesso, di volergli tutti e tre sodisfare; e segretamente ad uno buono maestro ne fece fare due altri, li quali sì furono simiglianti al primiero, che esso medesimo che fatti gli avea fare appena conosceva qual si fosse il vero.

The worthy man, who loved them all alike and knew not himself how to choose which one he ought to leave the ring to, considered that, having promised it to each one of them, he should like to satisfy all three; and in secret he had a master craftsman make two other rings which were so similar to the first that he himself, who had ordered them made, scarcely knew which was the true.

—Boccaccio, *The Decameron,* Day i, Third Novella

A STRANGER ARRIVES in an unknown city after a long voyage. He has been separated from his family for some time; somewhere there is a wife, perhaps a child. The journey has been a troubled one, and the stranger is tired. He stops before the building that is to be his home and then begins walking toward it: the final short leg of the improbably meandering way that has led him here. Slowly, he makes his progress through the arch that yawns before him, soon growing indistinguishable from its darkness, like a character in a myth disappearing into the jaws of some fabulous monster, or into the barren sea. He moves with difficulty, his shoulders hunched by the weight of the bags he is carrying. Their contents are everything he owns, now. He has had to pack quickly. What do they contain? Why has he come?

FOR A PERIOD of several years early in the new century I was working on a book the research for which required me to travel extensively throughout the United States, Eastern Europe, Scandinavia, Israel, and Australia. I went to those places in order to interview a number of survivors of, and witnesses to, certain events that took place during the Second World War in a small eastern Polish town where some relatives of mine had lived. These relatives were ordinary people, of little interest to history but nonetheless the focus, the center so to speak, of the story I wanted to tell, about who they had been and how they had died; just as the town itself, a place of little historical importance, had yet been the focus of my relatives' lives, the fixed point from which they had never wanted to stray. And so they died there, some hidden quite close to the house where they had lived, only to be betrayed; some rounded up and shot in the town square or in the old cemetery nearby; some transported to remote locales and then gassed. From this small place the few survivors would later radiate outward, after the war was over, to distant parts of the world — places that, only fifteen years earlier, would have struck these townspeople as improbable, absurd even, as destinations, let alone as places to live: Copenhagen, Tashkent, Stockholm, Brooklyn, Minsk, Beer Shevah, Bondi Beach. Those were the places I had to go, sixty years later, in order to talk to the survivors and hear the tales they had to tell about my relatives. The only way to get to the center of my story was by means of elaborate detours to distant peripheries.

When I was finished writing the story I found myself unable to move. At the time, I told myself that I was merely tired; but now the distance of a decade and a half permits me to see that I had experienced a crisis of some kind, even a kind of breakdown. For some months I found it hard to leave my apartment, let alone to do any traveling. I had been to Australia and Denmark and Ukraine, Israel and Poland and Sweden, been to the mass graves and to the museums, including one in Tel Aviv where, to my surprise, the thing that moved me most was a room full of meticulous models of synagogues that had, over the millennia, been built throughout the territory of the Jewish diaspora: in Kaifeng, China, and in Cochin, India, the sixth-century Beth Alpha Synagogue in Lower Galilee and the twelfth-century Santa Maria la Blanca Synagogue in Toledo (which owes its strange name to the fact that, shortly after it was built by a special dispensation from King Alphonso X to create "the largest and most beautiful synagogue in Spain," it was attacked by mobs, partly destroyed, and subsequently reconstituted as a church dedicated to the Virgin); the nineteenth-century Tempio Israelitico in Florence and its contemporary the Oranienburger Straße Synagogue in Berlin, both largely destroyed by fire in 1938 and now painstakingly re-created in miniature in Israel, a country that did not exist when those buildings were gutted. I was so moved, I think, because at one point from late childhood to early adolescence I myself had been an obsessive model-builder, carefully constructing precise scale replicas of ancient buildings, the mortuary temple of Egyptian pharaoh Hatshepsut in Deir el-Bahri, the Parthenon in Athens, Rome's Circus Maximus, each of those structures characterized, as I can now see although I doubt I was conscious of it at the time, by the insistent reduplication of a given structural or decorative element: ramps, columns, arches. I suppose I found the repetition reassuring. At any event, this is why, as I stood there in the model room of the museum in Tel Aviv, halfway through the worldwide journey I undertook in the early 2000s, I had such a strong emotional reaction. I was familiar with the impulse to make such replicas, which is haunted by a poignant paradox: the belief in our ability to re-create and the acknowledgment that the original has been lost . . . "Lost," I should say, can be a misleading word, implying as it does destruction beyond the point where reconstruction is possible. But there are other kinds of loss, alterations or repurposings of structures so extensive or dramatic that, although the

original still stands, is still present, we might nonetheless
feel the need for reconstruction of the sort to be found in
the Model Room at Beth Hatefusoth in Tel Aviv. There is,
for example, a decaying but still handsome structure that
dominates the market square of a small sub-Carpathian
town called Bolekhiv, currently located within the borders
of Ukraine although it was part of Poland when my relatives, who called it Bolechów, lived there, as their relatives
before them had done for many centuries until 1943, when
the last of them perished. This large rectangular building,
its pale pink stucco walls pierced at regular intervals by a
series of elegant tall windows with rounded tops, was once
known as the "Great" Synagogue of the town—a slight
pretension that can be forgiven when you consider, first,
that there were at one time more than a dozen synagogues
of various sizes in this small market town, and, second,
that most of the other buildings in Bolechów were in fact
quite small in comparison. The epithet "Great" can, if anything, strike you as poignant now, given that there is not
a single synagogue left in that place and that every single
person who ever attended those houses of worship, every
person who ever familiarly referred to this structure as
the Great Synagogue, is long since dead; and that almost
none of the people who live there now are aware that it
was once a place of worship. This is not surprising. In the
1950s, long before the vast majority of the current residents
lived there, the building had been converted into a meet-
ing house for leather-workers, its walls painted with murals
celebrating the landscapes of the Ukrainian Soviet Social-
ist Republic, and a decade before that the ark of the Torah,

once the focal point of its architecture, had been ripped out, its scrolls defiled and lost, its decorations stripped off. Hence although you could say that the Great Synagogue of Bolechów still stands, it seems nonetheless to have been "lost," seems to be in need of a model that could show you what it looked like when it was first constructed, the product of a living civilization. The historical reality which a model of an old building is meant to suggest is, therefore, more than merely material; such a model is surely meant to capture the (as it were) soul as well as the appearance of a building . . . But all this is a dream. There is no model of the Bolechów synagogue in the Beth Hatefusoth Museum, partly because no one who could help reconstruct its lost reality is alive today, and partly because if the museum were to re-create in miniature every synagogue in every town in Eastern Europe that suffered the same fate as the synagogue in Bolechów, it would take up acres, rather than a single room, in Tel Aviv.

The trip to the Model Room was the only occasion when I cried during my travels. Later, during the period of immobility that followed my return home, I would sometimes find myself in the middle of a room, looking around, unable to remember why I had entered it; standing perplexed in this way, motionless, I would burst into tears. A psychiatrist friend of mine suggested at the time that I was experiencing a kind of post-traumatic event. Having listened to tales of violence and destruction for five years without being able to assimilate them emotionally (because at the time I was listening to them my only thought was to "get the story down"), I was now, my friend surmised, having a delayed reaction. It was here, back in the familiar space of my home, that (she said) I was "doing my grieving." Whatever the reason, I felt emptied, emotionally and creatively. Every time I tried to begin a new project it was as if I had become one of the elderly witnesses or survivors I'd written about: a vacant wanderer arrived at last at a blank new place, unable to go on.

This strange state persisted for some time after I returned from my final research trip, which I took in July of 2005 and which brought me at one point to eastern Poland, where I saw the newly opened memorial of the Belzec death camp. It is a striking monument which is, so to speak, all periphery and no center. The memorial itself consists of a vast field where a large part of the camp had been situated. (The word "camp" can have misleading connotations. Belzec was a death camp, not a labor camp, which means it had no barracks, no sleeping quarters, nothing to suggest a habitation: you got off the train, as a great-aunt of mine did in September 1942, walked through the narrow passage known as *der Schlauch,* the hose, and went to the gas chamber.) This field has now been filled with stones of varying sizes, some of them as big as boulders, others as small as pebbles, that appear to have been burned. This impressively enormous space, with its suggestive barrenness—we understand that it is a place where nothing will ever live or grow—is in fact off-limits to the visitor; the commemorative act consists of walking around it. A paved path goes all the way round the field of burnt stones. Attached to this pavement are bronze letters and numbers, which also appear to have been burned, or perhaps badly rusted, and which spell out the names of every city and town in Europe from which a transport of human cargo went to Belzec, and the date or dates on which these transports took place. To walk along this path is, then, to retrace the history of Belzec as a killing field. Because many municipalities, even small towns such as the one I was writing about, had more than one transport to this death camp, and because the creators of this monument had decided that the names of the towns and cities should appear as many times as there were transports from those places, in the correct chronological order, there are certain place-names that appear and then reappear as you progress from MARCH 1942, the month of the first transport, to JUNE 1943, the month of the last— a scant fifteen months in which, nonetheless, six hundred thousand people were gassed—the foreign syllables becoming increasingly familiar, so that you almost find yourself looking for them, much in the way that certain characters or motifs in a play or a novel will make their mysterious entrances only to lose, as you keep watching or reading, their strangeness and become, finally, recognizable. The walk around the perimeter of the field is tiring.

That was, as I have said, in 2005. In 2008, on the advice of a friend who suggested that I return to what she called my "intellectual roots," I began to entertain the idea of writing something about the Greek classics. Although at first I was still incapable of beginning a new book, the idea of writing on a purely literary subject, on something whose charm and inventiveness, whose fantastical characters and settings and intricate construction would beguile and distract my still-bruised mind, appealed to me more and more as the months and then years passed. Wherever else it might lead, I thought, this Greek, this literary subject would at least allow me to leave behind the anguishing stories that had haunted me for so long and, in time, immobilized me: the tales of political collapse and religious intolerance, of escapes both successful and failed, of displacement and refugees, Germans and Jews. Soon after my friend shared her thought with me, the long period of morbid inaction I had been experiencing began to yield to one of reading and animated contemplation until, toward the end of that first decade of the century, for reasons I ended up describing in the book that I eventually wrote, it became clear what my subject would be. I decided to write a book about the *Odyssey*.

AS IT TURNED OUT, the book was difficult to write: so difficult that there were many occasions when I thought of abandoning it. I was baffled, balked: like some enchanted character in an old tale, the story I wanted to tell kept changing shape, shifting away from me, slipping from my grasp. The problems I was having with the Greek book were not at all like those I had experienced while writing the Holocaust book. The emotional despair that had characterized my relation to that book had yielded, in the new project, to what I can only call narrative despair.

Although there was a period when I studied Classics at the highest level, the book I was trying to write was not a scholarly work. It is, rather, about the last year of my father's life, which turned out, strangely enough, to be refracted through the *Odyssey*. In January of 2011, at the age of eighty-one, my father had decided to sit in on a first-year seminar on the epic that I was teaching, an experience that, despite the comic potential of the situation, had a profound impact on him, the students, and myself. In June of that year, just after the course ended, we heard about a Mediterranean cruise that purported to re-create Odysseus's voyages. We decided to take it, and the voyage turned out to be an experience during which a transformation of sorts took place in my father, a metamorphosis into a version of himself I had never glimpsed during our lives together. Then, in the autumn of the same year, he fell in a parking lot and suffered an injury that, in time, led to a massive stroke and, in still more time, to his death.

These experiences were profound, both intellectually and emotionally. But it was neither their depth and complexity, nor the awkwardness of some of the feelings that would rise to the surface in the classroom or the stateroom or the intensive-care unit, that baffled me, made the writing so difficult. The problem, as would become clearer as a year of writing became two and then three, was that I had no idea how to organize the story.

I had begun writing in the fall of 2012, six months after my father died, and by the end of August 2016, I had six hundred manuscript pages. Each of the three sections had been written, the classroom and the ship and the hospital, and yet the narrative as a whole wasn't working; reading through it was strangely tiring. As the summer came to an end and I despaired increasingly of finding a way to make the narrative work, I decided to seek out a friend of mine, an editor who has been a mentor to me since I began writing, nearly thirty years ago. I gave him the manuscript, and within a day he called me. The problem, this mentor of mine said, was that I had all the pieces but they hadn't yet come together. There was something wrong about the way I was telling the story, he went on; it was one thing after another, the seminar, the cruise, the illness and death. There was a lot of incident but it wasn't yet a *story*. The first part, the account of the seminar, was interesting (he observed, after a small silence during which I absorbed his criticism), but in his opinion the problem was that once you reach the end of that part—once you come to the end of the *Odyssey* course—you didn't want to keep reading. You don't want to get through the whole semester and then have to go on a *cruise,* he said, at which I weakly protested, But that's how it happened. I don't care how it happened, he returned, this isn't about fact, this is about a story. You need to find a way to plant the cruise and the hospital within the narrative of the seminar. Use flashbacks, use flash-forwards, don't worry about chronology. Make it up, if you have to! You just have to find a way.

When he said the word *way* I couldn't repress an embarrassed start of recognition. The phrase "find a way" allowed me, first of all, to understand retroactively the nature of the creative and spiritual crisis I had undergone after finishing my previous book. I was suffering from what the Greeks called *aporia:* a helpless, immobilized confusion, a lack of resources to find one's way out of a problem. The literal meaning of *aporia* is "a lack of a path," or "no-way." I hadn't been able to leave my apartment; I couldn't think of a new project. I was, in the Greek way of thinking, pathless—the adjective, as it happens, that, in the *Odyssey,* is used to describe the sea, the terrifying blank nothingness from which Odysseus must extricate himself, literally and figuratively, in order to reclaim his identity and find his way home.

The second thing that occurred to me after my conversation with my mentor was that the technique he was recommending—the insertion within one story of other stories, the flash backward or forward in time in order to give depth and complexity to the primary narrative—is one I have known about since at least my junior year in college, when I attended a seminar on the *Odyssey,* since this device is most famously used to great effect by Homer himself.

The technique is known as ring composition. In ring composition, the narrative appears to meander away into a digression (the point of departure from the main narrative being marked by a formulaic line or stock scene), although the digression, the ostensible straying, turns out in the end to be a circle, since the narration will return to the precise point in the action from which it had strayed, that return marked by the repetition of the very formulaic line or scene that had indicated the point of departure. The material encompassed by such rings could be a single self-contained digression or a more elaborate series of interlocked narratives, each nested within another in the manner of Chinese boxes or Russian dolls. This, at least, was the argument of a Dutch scholar named W. A. A. Van Otterlo, who in the middle of the last century published a number of studies of this widely wandering literary technique, culminating in a book called *De Ringcompositie als Opbouwprincipe in de epische Gedichten van Homerus,* "Ring

Composition as Structuring Principle in the Epic Poems of Homer," which would become the definitive scholarly statement on the subject. My editor friend had recommended the latter, more complex approach, although as a non-specialist he could hardly have been familiar with Van Otterlo's works, most of which were published during the Nazi occupation of the Netherlands, in 1944 and 1945, the years in which my relatives were trapped in their hiding places, or in places much worse.

I had known about ring composition during my university years. And yet, thirty years later, I had somehow managed to produce a book about Homer's epic, about teaching Homer's epic, a book that actually talks about this convoluted manner of composing, without internalizing its lessons. Now I knew at once what to do. I began rejiggering my manuscript in just the way my friend had recommended, folding episodes into one another, involuting certain narratives into larger story lines. The story of our marvelous cruise ended up curled inside an account of our seminar's reading of Books 9 through 12, the books of the *Odyssey* in which Odysseus relates his voyages and adventures; the story of my father's illness and death now spiraled outward from our class discussion about the climactic section of the epic, in which the hero is reunited with his family, his son and then his wife and finally his father; a section saturated with themes of identity, of startling physical transformations and long-delayed and emotional recognitions, themes I was reminded of more than once as I sat by my father's bed in the ICU, wondering, as people do who attend this kind of sickbed, whether the person by whose side I sat was in fact the person I had once known.

A STRANGER ARRIVES in an unknown city after a long voyage. He is middle-aged, and has been separated from his family; somewhere there is a wife, somewhere a child. The journey has been winding and the stranger is tired. He glances up at the building that is to be his home and, perhaps with a little sigh, begins walking toward it: the final short leg of the improbably meandering way that has led him here. There are stairs leading up to the building, which he mounts effortfully. Or maybe there is an arch at the entry to the building through which he now makes a sluggish progress, a small smudge disappearing into the gaping darkness. His shoulders are likely hunched by the weight of the bags he is carrying, the two bags which now are everything he has, apart from the wife and the child. When are they coming? The bags were packed in haste. What to take, what is most precious? One of them may well contain books.

Who is he? He could be anyone in the past half century: a Syrian, a Bosnian, a Kurd, an Angolan, a Ugandan. A few decades before that he would likely have been a Jew, a mild middle-European, say, who suddenly finds himself in some faraway city that would have been unimaginable in the life that was, until recently, his: Shanghai, Tashkent, Chicago, Istanbul . . . Istanbul. By the late 1930s the influx of German scholars to the Republic of Turkey is so heavy that the Minister of Education there allows himself a little joke: This immigration of Europeans to Istanbul, the Minister says, is a belated recompense for all the Greek scribes and poets and philologists who, hundreds of years earlier, had fled Constantinople for Europe as the Byzantine Empire collapsed under pressure from the Ottomans. So the Turk had joked in 1935. Two and a half centuries earlier this wanderer could have been a Huguenot. It is, let us say, 1685, the year in which the Edict of Nantes, the 1598 decree that had established toleration for French Protestants, was revoked, and this Frenchman, having fled his home and made an arduous journey by sea or land, now finds himself in one of the several nations that have welcomed the sudden great exodus of their Protestant brethren: England, the Netherlands, the German states. By 1689 there are so many French refugees in Prussia that the school built for their children in Berlin by the generous Friedrich Wilhelm, elector of Brandenburg and Duke of Prussia, is known as the *Lycée Français,* the French school, a name that it will retain long after anyone remembers its origin. Two centuries earlier still, in 1492, this stranger could be one of the tens of thousands of Jews and Muslims who, following the promulgation of the Alhambra Edict by the Spanish rulers Ferdinand and Isabella in July of that year, were forced out of Spain and eventually made their way eastward, to Istanbul. In the early 1490s the spate of non-Catholics, so many of them prosperous and productive citizens, rushing from west to east was so great that in Istanbul the Sultan, Bayazid II, allowed himself a little joke at the expense of his Iberian rival. "You venture to call Ferdinand a wise ruler," Bayazid laughed before his courtiers, "he who has impoverished his own country and enriched mine!"

Or it could be half a century still earlier. It could be 1453, and our weary refugee is now one of the many scholars about whom, five centuries later, the Minister of Education would make his jest: those scholars who, after Byzantium finally fell to the Ottoman Muslims in 1453 and the great capital was taken, were forced to flee westward, most of them to Italy, where the torrent of Greek-speaking scholars is so swollen that the nature of knowledge itself eventually shifted, as Greek became part of the mind of Europe for the first time in a millennium. He could be Janus Lascaris, for instance, the scion of an aristocratic Athenian family who was a boy of eight when Constantinople fell and who eventually ended up in Venice as a great scholar of Greek literature, a man who had a hand in many crucial intellectual undertakings of the time, from publishing the *editio princeps,* the first printed edition, of Aristotle's *Poetics* to annotating the text of the ten-volume *Histories* of Laonikos Chalkokondyles—this Chalkokondyles being another Greek who was displaced by the fall of the Byzantine capital, and who in those *Histories* described the last rotting century and a half of Byzantium up to and including the city's fateful fall; the description of which would, of course, have been all too familiar to his countryman Jan Lascaris as he read Chalkokondyles's *Histories* and, with what emotion we can only guess, made his meticulous scholarly notes in its margins. Or it could have been Chalkokondyles's brother Demetrios, who was born in Athens in 1423 but who ended up in Florence, another refugee from the Turks, where he became a great teacher, and where, in 1488, he published Ἡ τοῦ Ὁμήρου ποίησις ἅπασα, *Hê tou Homêrou poiêsis hapasa,* "the complete poetry of Homer": the *editio princeps* of the *Iliad* and *Odyssey.*

These were just three among the many dozens who fled the collapse of Byzantium, bringing with them their families and their precious baggage of manuscripts and the many-syllabled names with their hard Greek consonants, which, when you read through them in the indices of certain books or in the online lists of "Greek Refugee Scholars in the Italian Renaissance"—the movement of these exiles being significant enough to warrant being memorialized in such indices and lists and Wikis—explode in the mouth with the crunch of candied violets, the Chalkokondyles brothers, of course, but also Manuel Chrysolaras, invited to emigrate to Florence by that city's wise Chancellor in a letter politely quoting Cicero on the superiority of Greek to Italian culture, who wrote the first Greek grammar to be used in western Europe; or Zacharias Kalliergi, who published the first Greek book to be printed in Rome, an edition of Pindar's Odes; or Andronikos Kallistos, who, after his escape from the fallen city, taught Aristotle to the French. The list is a long one.

But the effects of the Fall of the City (as the Byzantines called their capital, since it needed no other identifier than that, *I Polis,* much as, half a millennium later, I, a child growing up in the suburbs of Manhattan, would ask my father to drive me into "the City" so I could stare at the huge scale model of the Parthenon that sat in a Plexiglas case outside the coat room of the Metropolitan Museum of Art on Fifth Avenue)—the effects of the Fall of the City rippled outward from the actual refugees. We need look only at the case of Demetrios Chalkokondyles to get a sense of the immensity of the impact that this upheaval, this Westward flow, had. To be sure, there was the publication of *The Complete Poetry of Homer,* a signal event in the history of the literature of the West. But there were also less material results of his flight from the East. For instance, there was the influence that this single displaced Greek, Demetrios Chalkokondyles, had on his students, one of whom was the German humanist Johann Reuchlin, among whose many accomplishments was the rather enlightened promotion of the study of Hebrew along with Greek and Latin in German schools; a pairing of the twin pillars of our civilization, the Greek and the Hebrew, Athens and Jerusalem, that to us now seems inevitable but that might have taken longer to seem inevitable had the Greeks not fled the victorious Ottoman Turks in 1453.

So our weary refugee could be any one of those Greeks. But he need not be a historical figure. Indeed, he could be the hero of the book that Demetrios Chalkokondyles published in Florence in 1488: he could be Odysseus. As Chalkokondyles supervised the setting of the Greek type for his momentous publication, how could he not have indulged in a wry smile? For the first line of the first book of the *Odyssey* could well be a description of Demetrios himself.

In this line we learn two crucial facts about Homer's hero. First, that he is *polytropos:* that is, "of many turns," an adjective that suggests not just the man himself, those twisty and convoluted habits of mind with which the stories that follow will make us so deliciously familiar, the seductions and tall tales and outright lies he is so good at fabricating, but also the painfully circuitous journey he must endure in order to reach his destination, a journey that more than once forces him to return to a place he has already been and start over: to travel in circles, in rings. And second, this line tells us that its hero was, like Demetrios, like those other Constantinopolitan scholars, "forced to wander very greatly," *mála pollá plánghthê:* in Odysseus's case, forced to wander greatly after he had sacked the sacred citadel of Troy, and in their case, forced to wander greatly after their city had been sacked. Some wanderers are less innocent than others . . . The Greek word *plangthê*, "wandered" or "roved," is a form of the verb *plazô*, whose range of meanings suggests the difficulties endured by the poem's hero. It can mean "to turn aside or away from," a sense that eventually evolved into another meaning, "to ward off," or to "baffle or balk," which evolved into yet another, figurative meaning, applicable to mental states: "to embarrass or trip up." The etymological intimation that there is something personally mortifying about all these detours and switchbacks and missteps is interesting—as if it were somehow the wanderer's fault that he wandered so widely.

But this exhausted wanderer could be someone else, too, someone who belongs neither to history nor to fiction. In his anxiousness, his irresolution and helplessness before this blank new façade, this figure becomes available as a type, as a very modern character. He could, for example, be a writer embarking on a new book.

THE BEST-KNOWN EXAMPLE of ring composition in Western literature is the carefully prepared and touching

passage in Book 19 of the *Odyssey* in which the hero is recognized by his old nurse Eurycleia. By this point in the
story, Odysseus has at long last returned to Ithaca. Aided
by his son, with whom he has finally been reunited, as well
as by some loyal servants, he has managed to sneak into
the palace disguised as a beggar, the better to be able to
assess the situation and contrive a way to kill the Suitors
and reclaim his wife. Not long after his arrival in the palace, the "beggar" is given a bath as a matter of traditional
courtesy; during this ritual the slave who has been given
the task of bathing him, an old woman long attached to the
royal household, notices a distinctive scar on this stranger's
thigh — a scar that, she well knows, marks him as none
other than Odysseus.

At this suspenseful moment the poet chooses not to
proceed to an emotional scene of reunion between the old
woman and her long-lost master. Instead, Homer brings
the narrative of that encounter to a halt as he begins to
circle back into the past, spinning the story of how Odysseus got his scar in the first place: of how, when he was a
youth newly grown to manhood, he was wounded in the
leg during a boar hunt that he participated in while visiting his mother's father, a notorious trickster and trouble-
maker called Autolycus. But this ring turns out to require
another, since (the author of the *Odyssey* assumes) we must
understand why Odysseus happened to be visiting his
grandfather in the first place. And so the poet traces a second circle, spiraling even further back in time to a moment
long before the boar hunt: the moment of Odysseus's birth.
Autolycus, we learn, had paid a visit to his daughter and her

husband just after their son was born, and it was during that visit that the baby's young nurse—the very woman who, in the "now" of the *Odyssey*'s primary narrative, recognizes the grown man as he sits in the bath—insisted that Autolycus be the one to name the newborn baby. In a fit of narcissistic preening, the grandfather who had caused so much pain to others gives his infant grandson a name best suited to himself: Odysseus, which is ultimately derived from the word *odynê,* pain. The hero of the complicated story has a complicated identity. He is *the man of pain,* one who suffers pain but causes others to suffer it, too.

From this crucial moment in the remote past the story winds its way gradually back to the surface again, stopping briefly to revisit the boar hunt before returning at last to the very moment when the now-elderly nurse recognizes the scar on the thigh of the beggar who has appeared in the palace at Ithaca: a moment that takes on added luster because we now have the history of the scar and its owner and his name. There, at the center of these concentric narrative circles, lies a key to the whole epic, the history of how the hero came to be himself, *polytropos.*

But *polytropos* was also a way to describe a certain literary style; was an attribute of texts as well as of persons.

In the twenty-third chapter of Aristotle's *Poetics,* the book that was helped into print by one of the many Byzantine Greeks who fled westward after the Fall of Constantinople, the Greek philosopher warns about some potential pitfalls in constructing the plots of epic poems. As examples of what can go wrong he uses two works, now lost, from the so-called Epic Cycle, the series of eight lengthy verse narratives which together related all the events having to do with the Trojan War, from its remotest prehistory—the wedding of Achilles's parents—to the final bizarre ramification of its most attenuated plotline: the accidental killing of Odysseus, in his old age, by his son Telegonus, his child by the witch Circe. Of that cycle, only the *Iliad* and the *Odyssey* remain, all of the others having fallen victim to the destructive force of time, neglect, fire, rats, and violence; manuscripts, after all, being only as safe as the libraries in which they reside, which is to say as safe as the cities in which the libraries reside, and as we know the cities of men are remarkably prone to destruction. Aristotle in the *Poetics* is particularly interested in what is wrong with two parts of the Epic Cycle: the *Cypria,* a rather haphazard affair that covered all the action from the nuptials of Peleus and Thetis to the Judgment of Paris to the abduction of the Greek queen Helen by the Trojan prince Paris, on through the first nine years of the war to the moment when Homer's *Iliad* begins; and the so-called *Little Iliad,* also something of a laundry list of a poem, narrating as it did much of the action after the death of Achilles up to and including the construction of the Trojan Horse and the Achaeans' terrible entry into Troy.

For Aristotle, both epics made the same fatal structural error. The structure of an epic, he writes, "should not be similar to that of histories, which require the exposition not of one *action,* but rather of all the events that happened during one *period.*" An "action," for him, is what we think of as "plot": a sequence of events whose elements are organically, coherently interconnected. A "period," by contrast, is merely a span of time during which a number of incidents take place one after another. Homer, Aristotle goes on to say, wisely avoided the historical method—that is, narrating sequentially every episode belonging to a given event (the Trojan War, in this case)—since this kind of serial structure "would be too extensive and impossible to grasp all at once." Instead, Homer wisely focused on "just one section" (as Aristotle puts it) of a larger event—that "one section," in the case of the *Iliad,* being the wrath of Achilles in the final year of the Trojan War, into which the poet artfully weaves a number of other episodes in order to give his composition what Aristotle calls "diversity." As examples of those other, less talented poets who failed to see the wisdom of Homer's method, Aristotle cites the poets of the *Cypria* and *Little Iliad,* who made the mistake of constructing their works out of many sequential actions in the order they occurred.

A mistake that I, too, once made, in the original version of my *Odyssey* book.

For all of its elaborations and narrative circling, the *Odyssey* is about what Aristotle calls "one complete action": the homecoming of Odysseus and everything that ramifies from it. Not the least of these ramifications is speculation about the nature of the hero himself, such speculation being the object of the poem's ring-like digressions and episodes: for instance, "The Scar of Odysseus" in Book 19. For this reason, digression is never the same as distraction. Its twists and turns are unified in their aim, which is to help us understand the one complete action that is the subject of the work to which they belong.

THE GREEK TASTE for the paradoxical way in which digression and what Aristotle calls "diversity" can enhance rather than detract from a given theme is evident in some ancient commentary on a crucial part of the *Odyssey*. In the third and fourth books of the epic, Odysseus's young son, Telemachus, is spurred by Athena, his father's divine protectress (who has assumed the appearance of an old family friend called Mentor) to leave Ithaca and seek information on his lost father's whereabouts, traveling first to Pylos (Book 3) and then to Sparta (Book 4) to interview his father's aging comrades, Nestor and Menelaus. Although these interviews turn up no hard evidence about his father's fate, most modern readers never question that the youth's voyages are, in and of themselves, somehow "educational"— that (like going away to college, say, or taking a gap year or a junior year abroad) the mere fact of leaving home and being on his own will play a crucial part in his maturation. Travel, we like to think — even getting lost now and then — is a good thing. Certainly there were scholars in ancient times who understood the boy's adventures in this way. One commentator on the *Odyssey* who was annotating line 284 of Book 1 (the line in which Athena, as she sets her ward's itinerary, advises him to "go first to Pylos and question godlike Nestor") argues that Telemachus's ensuing travels are "educational," and will moreover give him "glory on account of the search for his father."

But some ancient readers of Homer questioned the pedagogical value of Athena's advice. "Preposterous," one sage harrumphed in his marginal note to line 284, noting that by going abroad, Telemachus leaves his home unprotected and his mother open to danger. Baffled by what they saw as the foolishness of the goddess's plan, this scholar and others who followed his lead advanced another explanation for Telemachus's trips abroad: a literary, stylistic explanation. This portion of the *Odyssey,* the critics theorized, was designed to provide entertaining "variety" in a story that, they argued, otherwise had very little. Added on to the story of Odysseus's homecoming, the adventures of his son, the youth's conversations with two great figures of the Trojan War, would prevent the epic from being too (as one commentator put it) "uniform."

The Greek word for "uniform" that this commentator used is *monotropos,* "having only one turn." His choice of words suggests that, for the ancient readers of Homer, the aim of the *Odyssey*'s narrative was to be as *polytropos,* "many-turned," as its hero. Which is to say, the way to avoid boring uniformity is to add more and more turns. "Since the *Odyssey* does not offer sufficient variety by itself," another scholar concluded, "he [Homer] has Telemachus travel to Sparta and Pylos, so that much of what happened at Troy can be narrated by Nestor and Menelaus, by means of digressions."

Now there are two ancient Greek words for "digression." The one used in this passage is *parekbasis,* which literally means "a going off to the side"; the other, which is almost identical, is *parekbolê,* literally "a casting something off to the side." Curiously, this second word for "digression," *parekbolê,* eventually became one of the technical terms in Ancient Greek for "scholarly commentary." Digression, commentary: it's actually not hard to see how this

happened. Part of the work of ancient scholars was to com-
pile and extract the observations of other, earlier scholars.
After a while, these ever-expanding compendia of marginal
references — accompanied, to be sure, by the observations
of the scholar who was doing the compiling — became
freestanding critical works in their own right: which is to
say, commentaries.

The word *parekbolê*, for example, appears (in its plural
form, *parekbolai*) in the titles of two important works by a
twelfth-century Greek Orthodox cleric and scholar named
Eustathius. The works in question were his *Commentaries
on Homer's Iliad* and the *Commentaries on Homer's Odyssey*,
Parekbolai eis tên tou Homêrou Iliada and *Parekbolai eis tên
tou Homêrou Odyssea*, which, in the standard modern print
edition, together comprise six volumes of densely printed
Greek text. Even by the august standards of his own era,
Eustathius was an impressive scholar. Acknowledged already by his peers to be the most learned man of his age,
he had a prodigious knowledge of Greek epic and lyric poetry, among other genres. But it was his work on Homer's
epics that won him lasting renown. It does him no injus-
tice to say that his immense and meticulous commentaries
are valued today less for the author's original insights into
the epics than for his many quotations of other, much earlier scholars — including the greatest scholars of antiquity,
the heads of the Library of Alexandria, the first profes-
sional scholars to devote themselves to studying Homer's
poems — whose works have since been lost and which survive only in Eustathius's citations of them . . . "Lost," it
should be said, is often a euphemism. Many ancient texts

that had been preserved through centuries of careful copying and recopying by Byzantine monks later fell victim to wanton destruction. Some of the most devastating acts of such destruction, it is worth noting, were inflicted on Byzantium, a Christian empire, not by the Muslims (as many people assume) but by the Christian armies of western Europe which, during the twelfth and thirteenth centuries, ravaged the cities of the Byzantine Empire, they being closer to Europe and easier targets than were the cities of the Levant, the nominal targets of these Crusaders' violent energies. Most scholars agree that some major classical works that are now lost to posterity were still extant before 1204, the year in which soldiers of the Fourth Crusade sacked Constantinople and destroyed much of the city, a blow from which the Empire never recovered politically and which prepared the way for the coup de grâce administered two centuries later by the Ottomans when they finally took Constantinople in 1453.

But that was not the only instance of this shocking Christian-on-Christian violence. A generation before 1204 there had been the Sack of Thessalonica by the Normans. This was in 1185. Luckily for history, that dreadful event was memorialized in a work called *The Sack of Thessalonica,* written soon afterward by that city's septuagenarian archbishop. This text is notable both for its precise descriptions of the horrific atrocities visited upon the city and its people and for its admirable literary polish — particularly the echoes of Homer's style and diction. The description of terrified citizens seeking sanctuary in a church as trembling "like sheaves of corn," for instance, borrows an image from the Book 23 of the *Iliad,* while an evocation of the sun rising over the fields on the day after the city's sack ("which however had no power to put an end to the night of death") echoes the first lines of Book 3 of the *Odyssey,* which describes the sunrise that greets Telemachus when he visits Nestor in Pylos during his educational trip abroad. But these verbal parallels should not surprise us, since the author of the *Sack of Thessalonica* was Eustathius, that city's archbishop and the scholar whose commentaries on Homer, those famous and important *parekbolai,* are so invaluable.

For the Greeks, then, the "commentary," a genre that we turn to for illumination, derived quite naturally from the "digression," something many of us think of as an irritation, an impediment to knowledge.

A MAN HAS ARRIVED in an unknown city after a long voyage. He is tired, middle-aged; wracked with anxieties about the wife and child from whom he has been separated. He stands now before a building whose architecture is slightly fantastical to his eye and whose as-yet unknown interior will be his home for years to come. Wearily, he begins to climb the stairs.

Who is he? He could be so many people, the Spaniard or the Jew, the Muslim or the Greek. He could be a refugee from the Christians' destruction of Thessalonica, returned home at last to start rebuilding; he could be a Byzantine scholar fleeing westward from the fall of Constantinople, of whom as we know there were so many. It could be someone more recent; it could be a Jew in the 1930s. Indeed it is. For it is neither 1204 nor 1453, now: it is, rather, the late summer of 1936, and the stranger pausing before his new life is a middle-aged German Jew who has been separated from his family. There is in fact a wife, there is in fact a child; we know that, a few months after this exhausted refugee arrives in his exotic new home, they will safely follow him. On this summer day he is in his mid-forties, but seems older. A number of photographs of him survive. He has a fine, intelligent face with heavy cheeks that never quite become jowls, balanced by a high forehead which seems to be racing back to meet the vanishing hairline; the dour effect of the strong nose, which ends sharply, and the wide, slightly frowning mouth is alleviated somewhat by the dark eyes which, with their heavily hooded lids, look kindly and a little bit tired: the eyes of a person who understands a great deal and says somewhat less. His journey has been winding, wearying. We know that he has passed through many cities: Berlin, Munich, Vienna, Budapest, Bucharest. He has settled into his new home here in Istanbul and today arrives for the first time at the building that will house the office where he can do his precious work. He begins walking toward the strangely ornate edifice, a "magnificent palace," as another refugee scholar, a friend of our wanderer, would later recall, "with views of the blue Sea of Marmara, with beadles at every door, but almost no books." There is a short flight of stairs leading up to the doorway, which he mounts effortlessly. His shoulders, it is not hard to imagine, are hunched by the weight of the bag he is carrying. We can guess what is inside. His friend, that other refugee scholar, whose name was Spitzer, and who had preceded this tired traveler to Turkey long before the trickle of scholars became a desperate eastward rush, had warned him about the libraries, which could not compare to those of the rich German universities the two had known so well, and from which they have recently been expelled. *Unfortunately, there were almost no books.* But they were safe. Our wanderer hoists the bag up the stairs to his new place of work.

He is Erich Auerbach, a German literary scholar. One day in the future, largely because of a vastly learned book that he will soon write, he will be referred to as "the father of Comparative Literature," but now he is known, by those who know him, as a scholar of the Romance literatures and of medieval literature particularly — above all the poetry of Dante, another exile, about whom he has written a book that earned him the chair in Romance Philology at the University of Marburg, the position that he has recently been forced to give up. And so, along with all those other lucky Germans, he now finds himself in Turkey, having been invited to join the faculty at the University of Istanbul as part of that country's ambitious plan to remake itself as a European nation: an invitation which he and many others would have scorned a scant five years earlier but which now they have eagerly accepted, given what is happening throughout Europe. We remember the education minister's sour joke.

It is in this magnificent and empty building with its turquoise views of the Sea of Marmara, that crucial body of water which divides Europe from Asia, that this great authority on European literature will write his greatest

work, a paean to the civilization of the continent that he
has just fled. The name of this work is *Mimesis: Dargestellte
Wirklichkeit in der abendländischen Literatur, Mimesis: The
Representation of Reality in Western Literature.* This massive
tome, on which he labors in peace, in Istanbul, all through
the mid-1940s — the very years, as it happens, during
which, in the occupied Netherlands, W. A. A. Van Otterlo
is publishing his definitive papers on ring composition —
ranges easily over the entire landscape of Western writing,
poetry and history and fiction, from its first chapter, which
contrasts the Greek with the biblical style of narration (that
seemingly inevitable pairing) to chapters on the Roman
historians Tacitus and Ammianus Marcellinus; from Greg-
ory of Tours in the Dark Ages to *The Song of Roland* in the
early Middle Ages, from Dante and Boccaccio in the four-
teenth century to Voltaire in the eighteenth and Stendhal
in the nineteenth, ending with Virginia Woolf and Marcel Proust, his contemporaries, in the twentieth. Each of
its twenty chapters begins with a long and, it is to be assumed, representative citation from the work in question,
sometimes a few paragraphs and sometimes an entire page
or two, first in the original language — Latin, Occitan,
Provençal, Italian, French, German, English — and then in
Auerbach's translation, each citation being followed by a
minutely close reading of the text, all leading to an insight
into how that text achieves its mimicry (which is what the
Greek word "mimesis" means) of reality — and of course
what it understands the reality of life to be.

The meticulous analytical technique that Auerbach
would use to re-create the meanings of past writers in

his book is representative of the branch of literary studies known as philology: literally, the "love of words" or "love of learning." Philology is, simply put, the study of written literature in its historical context. When it began its existence as a formal academic discipline in the late eighteenth century, founded by a German called Friedrich August Wolf—a groundbreaking scholar of Homer's poems, as it happens—philology was intended to be as rigorous as any branch of the natural and physical sciences, which at that time were coming into great esteem. Literature, the interpretation of which many people casually think of as subjective, impressionistic, a matter of opinion, was, for the early philologists, an object like any other object of scientific enquiry: gravity, plants, stars. To understand the meaning of a literary text, one had to master its various elements, just as one had to master addition or trigonometry or the calculus in order to engage in higher mathematics; those elements being, in the case of literature, not only the language in which the text was written, its grammars and syntaxes and vocabularies, but also the history, religion, sociology, and politics of the civilization that produced the text.

As painstaking as its methods are, the overall project of this discipline is, if anything, almost touchingly grandiose: to construct a kind of model of the mind of the past, using the fragments and scraps and quotations of texts that have been left behind to recuperate the wholeness that was once there; to reproduce (as Auerbach put it) the entire "inner history" of a given culture, which seems in retrospect to have "proceeded as if according to a plan"—a plan that is perceptible only in retrospect because its contours are often obscured during the "twisted course" of history, the medium in which literature arises. Just so do the overarching themes and meaning of an epic or novel we are reading often elude our full comprehension until we finish it, when at last incidents or characters or motifs that may have struck us as casual or incidental when we first encountered them are revealed as having a significant, even a crucial place in the overall structure.

The philological method that is everywhere on display in Auerbach's *Mimesis* was something he had learned in his native Germany, a country renowned for the thoroughness of its scholarly tradition. Auerbach, who was born in Berlin in the late autumn of 1892 and was, therefore, forty-three at the time he arrived in Istanbul in the summer of 1936, had first been exposed to that tradition as a boy during the first decade of the last century, when, sitting in the safety of his schoolroom, he could hardly have been expected to imagine the religious and political persecutions that would come. His future had, no doubt, seemed cloudless back in the first years of the 1900s, when he was a prize-winning student at the Französisches Gymnasium in Berlin, the Lycée Français, where he was drilled in Greek and Latin and French — the germ, no doubt, of his scholarly inclination. And yet he realized his dreams only after a series of distractions and digressions: the First World War, in which he received a serious wound in the foot that left him with a scar for life; then an abortive career in the law, followed by a stint as a librarian. It was only in his mid-thirties that he found his calling, wrote his Dante book, and got his chair in Romance Languages.

From that early life, the rigorous training at the Lycée

Français and the varied and cosmopolitan exposure to the world that followed, would spring Auerbach's later and somewhat quixotic belief that philology, that painstaking excavation of a given literature's relationship to the historical moment that produced it, nonetheless held the key to the grandest plan of all: *die gemeinsame Verbindung der Kulturen,* "the common connectedness of all cultures." A number of scholars today, in fact, see *Mimesis* as a desperate if noble attempt to reconcile two incompatible impulses: the passion for philology, with its maniacal insistence on method and specificity, and the intuitive, vaguely Romantic human "feeling" (as the author once referred to it) that transcends the specifics of cultures and histories.

This concept of a universal literature of the human spirit was not new, as Auerbach himself acknowledged. He owed the idea to his countryman Goethe, who a century earlier had coined the term *Weltliteratur,* a literature of the world: a notion with an interesting genealogy that is linked, as it happens, to Istanbul.

Goethe came to his expansive humanistic vision of literature during the first two decades of the nineteenth century, a period in which his poetry was drawing inspiration from the East—particularly from the great verse collection, or *diwan,* of the fourteenth-century Persian writer Shams al-Din Hafiz, who is still considered the greatest of all Persian lyric poets and whose work, when Goethe encountered it, had been recently translated into German. The translator, an Austrian named Joseph von Hammer, was a diplomat who had stumbled into a literary career. After being posted to Istanbul, in 1799, he had fallen in love with the East, a consuming passion that eventually led him to write extensively about the Levant and its cultures after his return to Europe. His writings included a number of translations: of verse, including of course the *diwan* of Hafiz, which would so impress Goethe, but also of prose — not least, the fascinating memoirs of the Turkish traveler Evliya Çelebi, whose record of a trip to Athens in 1667 affords us a precious contemporary description of that city and its buildings, among others the Parthenon, which suffered devastating damage barely twenty years after he visited. There were also a number of learned treatises, with subjects as varied as the history of Constantinople (which is to say, Istanbul) and a study of assassins; his ten-volume *History of the Ottoman Empire,* for many years the standard work on that subject, was often compared to Gibbon's *Decline and Fall of the Roman Empire.* But it was von Hammer's translation of Hafiz, embedded in a study of Persian poetry, that would have the greatest impact, because of Hafiz's influence on Goethe, who in turn so strongly influenced the literature of the centuries to come. Hafiz's poetry made Goethe feel (as he wrote to a friend at the time) as though he were oscillating between West and East. This unifying movement between seemingly unbridgeable poles was reflected in the title of what many scholars agree was Goethe's last great collection of love poems, *West-Östlicher Diwan,* "The West-Eastern Diwan," written in the second half of the 1810s and published in 1819.

It was this dream of a fusion between East and West, born of his exposure to von Hammer's translation, that would lead Goethe, a few years later, to the concept of *Weltliteratur.*

The same vision underpins *Mimesis.* However disparate

the national cultures that the individual chapters analyze in such exhaustive detail, however specific the contexts in which those cultures' literatures must be understood and analyzed, Auerbach assumes that certain realities are, in the end, shared by all humans. There is a "common fate" that arises from a "diverse background," as he wrote in an article published a few years before he died, in a nursing home outside of New Haven, Connecticut: the last of his many destinations. It was a concept that he clung to with a tenacity you can only call poignant, given the specific history of his own times.

MIMESIS IS A WORK that is of interest to readers of the *Odyssey* for a number of reasons, one of them being the book's first chapter, which is called "Odysseus's Scar." In this introductory section, which establishes the methodological and intellectual bases for the critical endeavor to follow and thus serves as the "starting point," as Auerbach put it, for the entire project, the author explicates the scene from Book 19 that I have mentioned. Because his study seeks to understand how literature makes reality feel real, what this chapter is really about is ring composition: a technique about which, as it turns out, Auerbach has some doubts.

In his account of the scene, Auerbach comments with something bordering on bemusement on the fact that the "digression," as he calls it, into Odysseus's past that is triggered by Eurycleia's recognition of the scar—the "ring" that gives us the history of the scar and of the man who bears it—is nearly as long as the narrative of the scene taking place in the present. "There are more than seventy lines of these verses" that make up the digression about the scar, he observes, going on to note that the "incident itself"— the recognition of the scar by the old nurse as Odysseus sits in his palace once more after twenty years abroad—is barely any longer: eighty lines long. "All is narrated," Auerbach writes, "with such a complete externalization of all the elements of the story and of their interconnections as to leave nothing in obscurity." As Auerbach surely knew, the Greeks themselves applauded what he calls externalization. In an ancient literary treatise called *On Style,* for instance, by an author known as Demetrius, another passage from Homer is singled out for praise in terms that uncannily anticipate Auerbach's words. This passage, from the twenty-first book of the *Iliad,* is an extended simile in which the movement of an enraged river-god who flows and surges in hot pursuit of that epic's hero, Achilles, is compared to a stream of water that surges powerfully through an irrigation ditch once a laborer has painstakingly cleared the ditch of debris. (The choice of this particular passage will have seemed natural to the Greeks, whose myths are full of highly symbolic bodies of water, not least streams and rivers—for instance the dreadful River Styx, in which Achilles, the limits of whose prowess are demonstrated in this very passage, was dipped by his mother in an attempt to make him invincible.) For Demetrius, the success of the simile derives from the exhaustiveness with which the poet evokes the homely scene to which the god's movement is compared: the peasant with his hoe, the pebbles that are washed away once the blockage is cleared, and so on. "Its vividness," the ancient Greek critic writes, "depends on the fact that all of the attendant circumstances are mentioned; nothing is left out."

Nothing left in obscurity, Auerbach had noted; *nothing is left out,* Demetrius had observed. But whereas the Greek critic admires Homer's manner, the exhaustiveness of epic's descriptive technique — the way in which objects and persons, scars and brooches and bows, slaves and masters, all have histories that (with sufficient narrative space) can be illuminated, explained, accounted for — can, as far as Auerbach is concerned, present an obstacle to a persuasive representation of reality. For Auerbach, obscurity is, paradoxically, an advantage in literary mimicry, *mimesis.*

He demonstrates his idea a little later on, when he compares the Greek technique to the manner of narration that we find in the Hebrew Bible — a manner exemplified, for him, by the story of the sacrifice of Isaac in Genesis 22:1–19:

And it came to pass after these things, that God did tempt Abraham, and said to him, Abraham! And he said, Behold, here I am. And he said, Take now thy son, thine only son Isaac, whom thou lovest, and get thee into the land of Moriah; and offer him there for a burnt offering upon one of the mountains which I will tell thee of. And Abraham rose up early in the morning, and saddled his ass, and took two of his young men with him, and Isaac his son, and clave the wood for the burnt offering, and rose up, and went unto the place of which God had told him. Then on the third day Abraham lifted up his eyes, and saw the place afar off . . .

The passage, Auerbach points out, is full of opacities, blanks. Where are the speakers? he wonders. Whence does God come, whence does he call Abraham? Why, the modern critic asks, are we not given the reasons for God's dreadful temptation of Abraham, his faithful servant? "We are not told," comes Auerbach's reply to his own question.

One detail on which he focuses his critical attention is the three days' journey that takes Abraham to the place where he is to sacrifice his son, a journey that, amazingly to Auerbach, and no doubt to many others who, willingly or not, have undertaken arduous voyages, receives no further description in the Hebrew text. We do not know where it is set, we have no description of the terrains traversed, the animals or attendants who accompanied the father and son — nothing except what Auerbach characterizes as "what is necessary to the purpose of the narrative." And yet the very lack of detailed illumination is, the author implies, productive, since it forces the reader to probe further, to think harder about the characters, their motivations, their interior lives. This (as it were) efficient opacity of the narrative, Auerbach goes on to observe, reflects the elusiveness of the Hebrew deity Himself. "Even their earlier God of the desert was not fixed in form and content. . . . The concept of God held by the Jews is less a cause than a symptom of their manner of comprehending and representing things." (It is difficult not to be struck by the author's use of the possessive pronoun "their" in this passage, as if he were not a Jew himself; this diction makes me, at least, wonder whether his interest in opacity is purely scholarly.)

Both the opaque style of narration and the elusive deity, that is to say, are recognizable products of the Hebrews' distinctive mentality, their *Geist:* precisely what philological analysis is meant to reveal.

And so Auerbach finds the narrative inscrutability in the text of Genesis persuasively realistic. Just as we do not in fact know everything about the events and people encountered in our lives—certainly not the way in which the ring composition in Book 19 of the *Odyssey* allows us to know them—so too with the biblical narrative, which grants us only partial vision and imperfect information and, because of its fragmentary nature, its imperfection, feels real.

THERE ARE VARIOUS WAYS to describe the two styles of narration that Auerbach contraposes as he begins his epic journey through the literature of the West—those two styles representing, not incidentally, the two cultural pillars of European civilization. The Homeric or Greek technique with which the great critic begins is what you might call the "optimistic" style. Like a brilliant light, flattening out shadows and contours, putting everything on the same level, past and present, history and legend, it implies that everything can be known, explained, accounted for. And then there is the densely shadowed Hebrew style, the pessimistic "way," with its acknowledgment that, like God himself, creation is never knowable, but can (as Auerbach went on to argue) only be subject to interpretation.

Interpretation. However glum its premise, Auerbach's argument invites him and every other critic and writer in history, including me, to do what we do, which is to fill in the blanks, model what is no longer there, or what is not apparent. And so the very unknowability of creation necessarily, paradoxically generates further creation — more text, which in turn will require more interpretation. This makes me wonder whether the pessimistic and optimistic styles are not, after all, opposites so much as complements, two aspects of the same complex phenomenon, each necessary to describing that phenomenon and each inextricable from the other — the way our understanding of the word "cave," say, is constituted by our being able to imagine both its characteristic hollows, its defining emptiness, and its smooth stone walls, the structure that contains the emptiness. The Hebrew way, in this reading, is what makes possible the Greek way, the two being not so much points at opposite ends of a line as arcs of a continuous circle.

All this, I should say, was quite different from what I remembered it being when, ten years ago now, in my moment of *aporia,* of narrative despair, I consulted *Mimesis* for the first time in many years in the hope of finding there some insight that could be useful in rescuing my book about the *Odyssey.* I had recalled Auerbach's first chapter as a glowing endorsement of the ring composition that I was determined to adopt on my mentor's recommendation, only to find there the German Jew's grave doubts about Homer's technique and its ability to represent reality in the textured way I was hoping to achieve. Still, it is hard for me to give up my confidence in the Greek way — in the perhaps superstitious belief that behind the apparent fragmentation and chaos of the world (and what better example of that than the history of classical scholarship?) it is possible to perceive a shape; perhaps even a plan.

Indeed, in an epilogue he appended to *Mimesis* some time after completing it, Auerbach admitted that it was, in fact, his exile, his eastward wandering across borders and nationalities and continents, that made possible his great study of *Weltliteratur* (or at least of the European world and its culture)—much of which, legend has it, he had to write from memory of the various texts, given the relatively meager collections of the libraries that he found on arriving at his strange destination, which as we know could not compare to those he had left behind. However difficult for him and his scholar friends, this dearth was the object of a witticism on the part of the dean of the University of Istanbul. "We don't bother with books," the dean had replied after Auerbach's friend Spitzer asked about the library's resources. "They burn." For some people interested in the twentieth century and its dark histories, this comment will bring to mind the words of yet another German, the Jewish-born nineteenth-century poet Heinrich Heine, who famously remarked that wherever books are burned, people will end up burning, too—although it is unlikely that he could have predicted the scale of the burning his countrymen would one day be able to achieve, incinerations that would, as we know, extend far beyond the borders of Germany, to places like Belzec.

"The book," Auerbach wrote in his epilogue to *Mimesis,*

was written during the war and at Istanbul, where the libraries are not well equipped for European studies. . . . I had to dispense with almost all periodicals . . . and in some cases with reliable critical editions of my texts. . . . It is quite possible that the book owes its existence to just this lack of a rich and specialized library. If it had been possible for me to acquaint myself with all the work that has been done on so many subjects, I might have never reached the point of writing.

That is where we will leave Auerbach for now: at the once unimaginably distant point to which he fled and where he began to write, there just beyond the edge of Europe, the weary stranger arrived at the remote periphery where he will compose his masterpiece about the center, about the canonical texts of the West. Liberated, as Dante had been, by his exile, he is now able to surrender himself to memories of his intellectual and cultural home, memories which, because of what is happening there, are the only materials from which he will be able to build his model: a museum of a civilization that has lost its identity.

2

THE EDUCATION OF YOUNG GIRLS

Denn gründen alle sich nicht auf Geschichte?
Geschrieben oder überliefert!—Und
Geschichte muss doch wohl allein auf Treu
Und Glauben angenommen werden?—Nicht?
Nun, wessen Treu und Glauben zieht man denn
Am Wenigsten in Zweifel? Doch der Seinen?

Are all of them alike not based on History?
Whether written or traditional!—And mustn't
History be accepted on Trust alone,
And on our beliefs? Is it not so?
Now, whose Trust and whose Beliefs would someone be
Least likely to doubt? Surely his own people's?

    —Lessing, *Nathan the Wise*

ERICH AUERBACH WROTE *Mimesis* during the mid-1940s, in Istanbul, safely hidden away from those who, back in his German homeland, would have hunted him to destruction—that metaphor, however melodramatic it may seem, being one that has been difficult for me to avoid since the period some fifteen years ago in which I was researching my book about the Holocaust, during which time, I well recall, one of the survivors whom I was interviewing shook his head in frustration over his inability to adequately convey to me the "feeling," as he put it, of being the object of German persecution. "You don't understand," this elderly Pole had said to me as we sat in the living room of his apartment in Bondi Beach, Australia. "One minute we were middle-class people, doing ordinary things. Take your uncle, for example! I remember how he with his four daughters was always complaining about the school fees—educating those girls wasn't cheap, I can tell you! And then the next minute we were being hunted like animals. Anyone could kill us, you see. You weren't a *person* anymore." Each day Auerbach would leave his home and go to work in the rather elaborate old mansion where the literature faculty of Istanbul University was now housed, the ornate edifice with its spectacular views of the Sea of Marmara, of which his friend Spitzer left his charming description even while deploring the University of Istanbul's lack of an adequate library. Meanwhile, W. A. A. Van Otterlo was working away in the Nazi-occupied Netherlands on the papers about Homeric ring composition that together were destined to become the definitive scholarly statement on this technique for generations—working, it should be said, under dire conditions that worsened as the war drew on, culminating in the "Hunger Winter" of 1944–45, or, as one Dutchman I interviewed called it, the "Tulip Winter," because during that season starving Dutchmen would dig up the bulbs of the flowers for which their country is famous and eat them. Of the varieties of ring composition that Van Otterlo analyzes in his work, there is one that he calls "inclusive." In the inclusive ring technique, a lengthy digression—a "more or less self-contained passage," as Van Otterlo puts it—is set inside a hollow or niche that has, as it were, been carved out of the main narrative, the opening of any such niche marked in the text by means of a certain formulaic line or scene that triggers the digression. Once the digressive passage has reached its conclusion, the line or scene is repeated to mark the closure of the circle, the completion of the ring.

My interest in circles, rings, and inclusive narratives of the kind that both Auerbach and Van Otterlo labored to analyze during the war years bemuses me, since the fact is that I have always had a horror of enclosures of any kind. There were certain games which, as a child, I found hard to play because they involved hiding in narrow spaces — closets, basements, the warm spot behind the furnace in the cellar that, for my siblings and cousins, was a favored spot for concealment during the games we sometimes played. Whenever I had to crouch in such spaces I would begin to sweat profusely and to breathe abnormally quickly, as the flesh along my neck tightened: the signs, as I would learn only later, of a panic attack. I am claustrophobic. On summer nights when I was twelve or thirteen or so, all of the neighborhood children my age and slightly older would play a game we called "monster tag," a version of hide-and-seek that would spread over the ten properties that constituted our neighborhood, five houses on one side of the street, together with their front and back yards, and five on the other, and which would involve all the neighborhood children who were willing to play. This game would begin just as the day was ending and the last glimmers of daylight were becoming indistinguishable from the first wash of evening — the time of day that the French charmingly if a bit mysteriously call *l'heure entre chien et loup,* the hour between dog and wolf. At the beginning of the game, some of us — it was always the same group of ten kids or so — who were called "hiders," were given a certain amount of time to conceal ourselves from the other children, who were called the "hunters." The hiders would cram themselves in porches and sheds and garden beds, fashioning ingeniously camouflaged blinds in the same way that, in real life, hunters do, using the ample vegetation that adorned the houses on our block, or squatting underneath lavish oak-leaf hydrangeas that were watered by crisscrossing hoses which snaked along the lawns in all directions, some parallel to one another, others looping back on themselves in huge circles; or, if the hiders were particularly fearless, wedged among the feathery cypresses that surrounded Mrs. Isaacson's property at the end of the street. These trees had been planted by her husband when all these houses were new, fifteen years earlier; since then, Mr. Isaacson had died but the cypresses had flourished, growing to obscure first the ground-floor windows and then the windows of the upper story of the Isaacson house, giving the place a furtive, even sinister air, as if the growth of the trees had been meant to obscure whatever was happening behind the blinded windows. But there was probably only the sorrow of the dark-haired widow and her gentle, tall son, Robbie, whom we would shyly greet every day in the late afternoon as he walked his enormous German shepherd, Lady, which, people said, was half wolf. Some time early in the 1970s, as I remember it, the town issued an order to take down Mrs. Isaacson's cypresses because they had created a dangerous blind spot for drivers making the turn at the bottom of our street, but she took the county government to court and made them replant the cypresses in a less dangerous configuration at their own expense, her argument being that, because her late husband had planted them, they constituted a memorial, and who would want to desecrate a memorial? For this reason, I associated cypresses with death during my childhood, never guessing, then, that there is in fact a long-standing cultural association between that species of tree and funerals, graves and cemeteries.

That association, as well as my fear of being enclosed, contributed to my intense aversion to our summer games of monster tag. Often when I was chosen to be one of the "hiders"—I was never a "hunter"—I would furtively make my way back to our house and go inside, deliciously freed of the responsibility to conceal myself. But of course, it is not always possible to free oneself from the obligation to enter small spaces. Since those childhood days, I have experienced moderate to extreme anxiety when required to be in certain closed environments: the cabins of small aircraft, MRI machines, elevators.

For this reason it is easy to imagine the horror I experienced when, at the end of the many travels I mentioned earlier, the investigative journeys I undertook when writing my book concerning the fates of my relatives during the Holocaust, I was able at last to locate the underground hiding-place in which two of those relatives, my great-uncle and one of his four daughters, had been concealed for a period of time, hidden by two neighbors after Bolechów was overrun by the Germans late in the summer of 1941—the beginning of the period when, as the survivor I interviewed had put it, Jews were being hunted down like animals by the Nazis and their local collaborators. When the hiding-place was revealed to me in July 2005—a subterranean chamber about eight feet below ground level, accessed by a trap door, measuring perhaps six by three feet—I naturally felt obligated to go down into it since this, I realized, was as close to a memorial as they would ever have, unlike their luckier American relatives who had emigrated from Poland before the war and all of whom now repose together in a vast Brooklyn necropolis called Cypress Hills. During the awful minute I spent down there where my uncle and his daughter had been hidden, it occurred to me to wonder whether claustrophobia, like certain other kinds of anxiety disorders, might have a genetic root, and hence whether, during the unknowable period of time that my two relatives were forced to hide, they had to endure, in addition to the other terrors they were suffering, the fear I knew so well.

Another occasion on which it was impossible to conceal my phobia was in June of 2011, when my father and I were on the *Odyssey* cruise. At a certain point we stopped at Malta, where, according to an old tradition, the nymph Calypso held Odysseus captive as her love-prisoner, turning him into a nobody, a man with no country or family or renown, by hiding him from all the world; such concealment no doubt having come to her naturally since her name is, after all, derived from the verb *kaluptein,* "to hide." This anonymizing captivity, according to Homer, went on for seven years until Zeus himself, yielding to the entreaties of Odysseus's divine patroness, Athena, sent his son Hermes down to Calypso's island with orders for the nymph to set her mortal lover free. The island is described as being in the middle of the sea, as far from humanity as one could imagine: *extremi hominum,* as one learned admirer of the *Odyssey* would put it many centuries later. Homer's description of the cave in which the hero's identity has been swallowed up goes well beyond the conventional and, it must be said, rather unimaginative adjective used for this and other caves in his epics: *glaphyros,* hollow. The first thing we hear about Calypso's home is in fact that it is *mega,* great, and the description that follows suggests that it was a capacious space scooped out of the living rock. This hollow, we learn, is filled with luxurious furnishings, heated by roaring fires whose aromatic smoke perfumes the whole island. Like Odysseus, whose prison this space is, the cave itself is "hidden," surrounded by cypresses and other trees, their branches filled with the nests of owls and other birds, the whole property watered by streams that crisscross meadows filled with violets and parsley and "flow with bright water hard by one another, turned one this way, one that." Despite the presence of some sinister elements — the nocturnal birds, the plantings of trees associated with death — the scene has an extravagant, wild beauty. It is a sight so gorgeous that even a god like Hermes, Homer says, can't help but admire it when he arrives, as dumbstruck as a mortal.

But in real life, as I discovered, the cave is tiny and its environs unremarkable at best and bleak at worst: a yellow-brown rockscape parched by the unrelenting sun, the baked stones cruelly hard on the sneakered feet of tourists such as the small group from our ship that, that June day in 2011, straggled down the thirsty embankment that led to the entrance of the cave. As we approached, a familiar clamminess began to prickle along my neck. The entrance itself couldn't have been more than two feet wide, a gash in the face of the rock. I stood there, refusing to go in, at which point my father, in an uncharacteristic display of physical affection, offered his hand to me, a gesture that so surprised me that I found myself taking comfort from it and acquiescing before I had time to ponder why he had done it. Hand in hand, we pushed our way through. But once I was inside the panic rose in my throat. The space inside is not *mega*. It was hard to imagine that this could have been the model for the opulent abode described in Homer's text. Out of an obscure sense of duty I lingered for a few seconds and then scrambled out — with precisely the same feeling of relief, I only later realized, that I had experienced a number of years earlier, in Ukraine, when

I emerged from the underground chamber in which my relatives had been forced to remain perfectly still for an amount of time we still do not know.

"CALYPSO WAS INCONSOLABLE after the departure of Ulysses," a famous text tells us about the aftermath of Odysseus's departure from her cave. The beauty of her island, this narrative goes on, "only brought to her mind the sad memory" of the departed hero. But the text I am quoting is not the *Odyssey,* which in fact has nothing to say about Calypso's feelings after the departure from her hollow cave of the lover to whom she had offered immortality if only he would remain with her; an offer that he refused. "Calypso was inconsolable after the departure of Ulysses" is, rather, the first sentence of a late seventeenth-century French novel that was based on the *Odyssey,* one of many literary adaptations over the centuries for which Homer's epic served as a model. What is curious about this text is its ingenious design: for although it invents a number of new episodes for Homer's characters, it is so constructed that these inventive digressions function as an insert into the text of Homer, one that in no way disturbs or interferes with the action of the original — as if the *Odyssey* itself were a cave, a series of vast hollows in which new digressions and narrations and adaptations could be hidden.

This technique is itself an ancient Greek one. For instance, in Herodotus's *Histories* of the Persian Wars — the wars waged by the Persian emperor Darius against a coalition of Greek city-states between 490 and 479 BC, the conflict that led to the famed Battles of Marathon and

Thermopylae — there is a book-length digression about the land of Egypt, its mores, histories, architecture, and manners. Why does Herodotus pause to provide this vast excursus? Because Egypt was part of the Persian Empire at the time of the wars, and for that reason was worthy, in the historian's eyes, of this fabulously lengthy narrative detour. *Nothing is left in obscurity.* The "Egyptian *logos*" (narration or tale), as it is known, is the largest by far of many narrative cul-de-sacs to be found in the *Histories,* each illuminating some aspect of the principal narrative, to which, eventually, it returns — although it must be said that for many modern readers Book 2, the Egyptian tale, is so long, so absorbing in its own right, that it becomes easy to forget about the Persians and their wars with the Greeks.

The novel that opens with a reference to Calypso was composed in the 1690s by a French churchman and theologian called François de Salignac de La Mothe-Fénelon. Born in 1651 into an aristocratic family who held their seat in the southwest of France, near the Périgord, Fénelon was the last of twelve children, and therefore destined from the start for a career in the church, a fate that rendered him ineligible for the dashing pursuits of various of his male relatives — a cousin, for instance, who died valiantly in 1669 as a member of the European forces aiding the Venetians at the Cretan stronghold of Candia, modern-day Iraklion, against the Ottoman Muslims who besieged that city for twenty-three years, the second-longest siege in recorded history, one that makes the Greeks' siege of Troy seem almost casual in comparison; or an older brother who distinguished himself while fighting against the Ottomans during the so-called Morean War in the 1680s, another of the many theaters in the "Great Turkish War," the seemingly endless conflict between the Christian Europe and the Ottoman Empire, West and East, that ran throughout the seventeenth century. However destructive it was, this confrontation between cultures seems at least to have fired the younger François's creativity. As one of Fénelon's biographers has put it, the Orient and Occident, seemingly opposite, came together as one in the imagination of the future author, *l'orient et l'occident se réunissent:* something that was not, it seems safe to say, happening in the real world.

While still a small child, as far as we can surmise, François was tutored at home in Latin and Greek, the latter language in particular having captured his fancy. He was ordained as a priest in 1677, at the age of twenty-six. Only two years later he attained his first major advancement, having been asked to run a school called the Institut des Nouvelles Catholiques, an institution whose curriculum was designed to educate as devout Catholics the wellborn daughters of Protestant parents who had recently converted to Catholicism. It is hard not to think that these girls' parents were wise, since just a few years after Fénelon took over at the Institut Louis XIV revoked the Edict of Nantes, that far-sighted decree which, not quite a century earlier, had established toleration for the Huguenots; as a result, the Protestant religions were banned and their practitioners subject to harassment, violence, and forced conversion. The foresight shown by the parents of Fénelon's charges at the Institut des Nouvelles Catholiques always makes me wonder about some people's capacity for a certain kind of prescience, an ability "to see the handwriting on the wall"—a phrase that became familiar to me over the years of my childhood and adolescence since it recurred in my family's ongoing and fruitless discussions of the decision-making processes, and ultimately the fates, of our relatives in Poland, who had, all too clearly, been unable to "see the handwriting on the wall," which is why they remained first in their small town and finally in those dark hiding places. I sometimes wish I had known, when I overheard these conversations as a child, the origin of this expression, since had I done so I might well have disputed my family's use of that particular term in the story of my relatives. For the phrase comes from the Book of Daniel, which relates how, at a great feast, the Babylonian King Belshazzar saw a disembodied hand writing on the wall of his palace as he drank from golden vessels that had been looted from the great Temple in Jerusalem by his father, Nebuchadnezzar, who had destroyed that temple and enslaved the Jews, forcing them into their long Babylonian exile. Belshazzar's wise men were unable to read the writing on the wall, but the Hebrew sage Daniel could, and saw that it was a message of impending doom: and indeed that very night Belshazzar was defeated and killed by the conquest-mad Persian emperor Darius . . . Had I known all this when I was a child, I would have pointed out that the inscrutable message in the Bible is intended for evil men, whereas our relatives had been innocent. Surely in their case, I like to think I would have argued, the handwriting should have been clearer, its meaning less opaque than it was to the unbelievers.

The French Protestants who hadn't seen the handwriting on the wall either stayed and suffered the consequences which I have mentioned or fled France for other countries: England, the Netherlands, and of course Prussia, where Duke Friedrich Wilhelm welcomed the weary and traumatized émigrés by building for them an educational institution of their own, the Französisches Gymnasium, the Lycée Français, where, so many years later, Erich Auerbach would learn Greek.

Fénelon's special interest in education was made evident in the publication of his *Treatise on the Education of Young Women,* published in 1687. That work, along with his other attainments and of course close friendships with important courtiers, one of whom, the duc de Beauvilliers, was responsible for the upbringing of the King's grandchildren, would help to earn the brilliant pedagogue-priest the greatest possible mark of esteem. Two years after the publication of the *Traité de l'éducation des filles* he was named tutor to the seven-year-old duc de Bourgogne, the Duke of Burgundy, the eldest grandson and, thus, eventual heir of the Sun King. It was for this boy that Fénelon—who, in recognition of his talents, to say nothing of his usefulness to the royal family, was eventually made an archbishop—began to compose a series of ethically instructive tales based on Homer's *Odyssey.* These were eventually collected and published in book form in 1699 as *Les aventures de Télémaque,* "The Adventures of Telemachus," the novel I referred to earlier, which begins with Calypso in her cave. This immensely popular work would earn its author lasting literary fame throughout the world, although it was also to seal his catastrophic fall from grace at Versailles.

Les aventures de Télémaque comprises eighteen chapters,

or "books." Its hero is Télémaque, Telemachus, the son of
Odysseus (or, as we must call that character here, *Ulysse*):
the young man who is also the hero of the first four books
of the *Odyssey,* the books in which the youth is inspired by
Athena to leave home for the first time and go abroad in
search of information about his long-lost father. In Homer's
epic, Telemachus sails home to Ithaca from Sparta, where
he has spent a strange evening listening to Helen of Troy
and Menelaus, the cuckolded husband to whom she has
long since been reconciled, as they reminisce about the war
in which they played such key roles. In Fénelon's expansion
of Homer's original, however, the young man seeks out
further adventures after his Spartan sojourn. Despite the
warnings of the companion whom Fénelon gives him —
a sage old man called Mentor, who is, in fact, Minerve,
Minerva, the Roman goddess of wisdom (Homer's Athena) in disguise — Télémaque insists on sailing to Sicily,
where he is nearly killed by Trojan refugees who still har-
bor a grudge against the Greeks. This is the first in a series
of dangerous adventures that, over time, educate the youth
in the ways of the world, in statesmanship and war-craft, in
friendship and loyalty, and which lead him, eventually, to
be shipwrecked on the island of the nymph Calypso. Télémaque's recitation of all that has befallen him — the narrow
escape from Sicily, captivity in Phoenicia and on Cyprus,
temptations by Venus, goddess of love, an adventure in
Crete, whose laws he studies and whose king, Idoménée,
serves as a model of bad kingship throughout Fénelon's
text — so enchants Calypso that she develops an obsessive
passion for him, which eventually drives him from her

island. Further adventures follow, each one leading to the enunciation of edifying morals about the dangers of greed, egotism, dishonesty, and erotic indulgence. It is only after he learns these lessons, after he understands that "a king is worthy of commanding and is happy in his power only inasmuch as he subjects it to reason," that Télémaque returns home to Ithaca at last.

In the episodes that make up the eponymous exploits of *Les aventures de Télémaque,* the erudite author self-consciously echoes details of the *Odyssey* in a way that is clearly designed to bring a knowing smile to the lips of connoisseurs of Homer. Calypso, for instance, is slyly transformed in the opening pages into a double of Homer's Odysseus. Just after Ulysse leaves her enchanted island, Fénelon writes, the nymph falls into a state of despondency, standing "immobile by the sea shore which she wetted with her tears; and she was always turned to face the shore where the vessel of Ulysse, braving the waves, had disappeared from her sight." Those familiar with Homer's poem will remember the first glimpse that the epic gives us of its hero, at the beginning of Book 5: "sitting by the seashore weeping, as was his wont, / Wracking his heart with tears and groans and grief. / He would gaze across the barren sea and shed his tears." But as the Frenchman's narrative progresses, it becomes clear that entire episodes from Homer's epics are being (as it were) remodeled. Like Achilles in Homer's *Iliad,* Télémaque receives a marvelous shield, described at great length and in exhaustive detail, that is fashioned for him by Vulcan, the blacksmith god; and like Odysseus in the *Odyssey,* the young hero endures a harrowing descent into the land of the dead, where he beholds a panoply of famous heroines and heroes whose sins or triumphs are the object of further instructive moralizing.

Still, for all the cunning resemblances, there are striking differences. Not the least of these is Fénelon's increasingly original portrayal of Calypso. In Homer, the nymph is rather sympathetic, showing admirable backbone when confronted with the gods' demand that she give up her lover — a divine order that, with equally admirable pragmatism, she chooses to obey. (As she does so, she articulates a startlingly modern complaint about the gods' double standard for sexual behavior: male divinities get to keep their mortal lovers, she complains, but goddesses always have to give theirs up.) But in *Les aventures de Télémaque,* this alluring and clear-eyed character becomes a symbol of female passions run amok, less a character from Greek epic than one of the heroines of the tragedies of Racine (a writer whom Fénelon knew): a vengeful, tormented, desire-maddened woman who will stoop to anything to punish the youth who has proved immune to her charms — and an exemplar, as no doubt even the young duc de Bourgogne could perceive, of the kind of female that virtuous young princes ought to avoid. Like Homer's Odysseus, who while proclaiming his fidelity to his wife all through the *Odyssey* nonetheless manages to slake his appetites for female companionship, Fénelon's text manages to display an allegiance to "home" while meandering far from it, the allegiance showcasing his literary erudition even as the meanderings constitute a tribute to his creative inventiveness.

It is difficult not to think of this business of wanderings and returns, of points of departure and distant divagations, when encountering a passage that comes early in Fénelon's tale: the description of Calypso's cave. In *Les aventures de Télémaque,* the nymph's abode is not concealed by funereal cypresses, as it is in Homer, but rather is conspicuously located on the slope of a hill, from one side of which can be seen the sea glittering below, while the other side looks out onto a stream dotted by islands. These islands, the author observes, are demarcated by canals

> which seemed to play amid the countryside: some rolling along swiftly with their clear waters, others with their placid, sleepy waters, and still others doubling back on themselves, by means of long detours, as if to return to their source, as though incapable of leaving those enchanted banks.

There are streams running near Calypso's cave in Homer, but these are barely described by the poet: "one turned this way, the other that." Fénelon's scene-setting is more elaborate. Given the twofold relation of the Frenchman's text to Homer's — at once imitative and inventive, both paralleling and diverging from its model — the canals in *Les aventures* begin to strike you as heavily symbolic. For narratives, too, move like streams. Some, as we know, roll along swiftly, while others barely move; still others, despite the lengthy detours they take, end up just where they started, yearning to return to their source.

That last stream in particular is interesting. In the earliest printed versions of *Les aventures de Télémaque,* the work is described as being the *suite du quatrième livre de l'Odyssée d'Homère,* the continuation of the fourth book of Homer's *Odyssey.* But *suite,* continuation, suggests an open-ended trajectory—a vector that moves, like the first of Fénelon's streams, rollingly and freely ahead; whereas the narrative in *Les aventures de Télémaque* turns out to have a very different shape. At the end of Homer's Book 4, Telemachus has come to the end of that memorable evening of storytelling and reminiscing by Menelaus and Helen; at this very moment the epic abandons him, turning first to the plotting of the Suitors and then to Odysseus, whom we meet at last in the next book, Book 5 (the very passage in which we see Odysseus weeping by the seashore). It is not until Book 15 that the son's story is picked up again, when we see him leaving Sparta on his way home to Ithaca: in the final lines of that book, Telemachus disembarks on an out-of-the-way shore of his native island and makes his way to the hut of the swineherd Eumaeus, where, in the next book, he will meet his father. It is within this enclosure hollowed out of the plot of the *Odyssey,* bounded by Book 4 on one side and the conclusion of Book 15 on the other, that all of the action of *Les aventures de Télémaque* take place. Which is to say that, inventive and digressive as it can be, Fénelon's novel ends by returning to its source, landing Télémaque exactly where he needs to be for the plot of Homer's poem to snap into place and lead the son to the father. And in fact, the climactic moment of father-son reunion described in Book 16 of the *Odyssey* is precisely where Fénelon's adaptation ends. In the closing lines of the archbishop's novel, Minerve gives her charge a final word of advice and then flies off, leaving Telemachus and his companions to return home to Ithaca where, according to the final sentence of Fénelon's novel, *il reconnut son père chez le fidèle Eumée,* he recognized his father in the home of the faithful Eumaeus.

And so what looks like a meandering plot in *Les aventures de Télémaque*—a series of incidents that, you often feel, could keep on going as long as the archbishop's capacity for invention remained unexhausted—is, in fact, a tightly bounded circle. As with the last of the streams that flow near Calypso's abode, there are wanderings, *longs détours;* but in the end they are not turnings-aside, *dé-tours,* but turnings toward—revolutions that bring us back to where we began, the *source:* in this case, the *Odyssey* itself, the wellspring of the narrative that Fénelon has ostensibly invented. Wherever it may lead, whatever fanciful inventions it contains, the archbishop's fantasia on Homeric themes points to the potentially infinite number of circles that can be drawn within a single ring.

ON THIS PSEUDO-ODYSSEAN armature Fénelon hung the ethically instructive material for which the book became famous—and, for himself, dangerous. At the close of the seventeenth century it did not require an Odysseus-like cleverness to discern in the text's many lectures (often put in the mouth of Minerve) on good kingship—to say nothing of the devastating portrayal of Idoménée, the Cretan king who, whatever his good intentions, is repeatedly criticized for his pride, his susceptibility to flattery, his vanity, and his penchant for expensive wars and costly luxuries— a bitter critique of the Sun King himself, who is alluded to at one point by means of a striking metaphor. "These great conquerors," a character observes, "always depicted so gloriously, resemble those rivers in spate that look majestic but which ravage the fertile lands they are meant simply to water." Louis, no fool, was enraged, and in 1699, soon after the novel was published, Fénelon was sent packing to the diocese of which he was titular head, far in the north of France, a bleak and cold place that was particularly hard on the aging southerner, who in a letter to a friend soon after he arrived at this unfriendly destination described himself as being *extremi hominum,* at the extremes of human habitation — "more Germany than France," as the archbishop bitterly put it. Meanwhile, at Versailles, his supporters at court mourned his absence. In a sympathetic account of the clergyman's disgrace, the diarist Saint-Simon compares the grief of Fénelon's friends at Versailles to the mourning of the ancient Jews for Jerusalem during the Babylonian Captivity, that period of exiled enslavement following the destruction of the Temple. The lamentations of Fénelon's partisans, their constant hope of his return, were compared by the diarist to "the way in which that unhappy people still wait for and sigh after the Messiah." In a portrait made before his downfall, the archbishop has an elongated but kindly face, the high hooked nose, with its sharp tip, and the rather pointed chin offset by the warm dark eyes, whose brows are raised in what can strike you as an attractive frankness — an openness to questions, to possibility, not always present in the faces of high clergymen. It is the patient and generous (if slightly weary) face of a good teacher. It is sad to think of this face gazing down at a sheet of paper on which the words *extremi hominum* have just been written.

Whatever irritation it may have caused Louis, *Les aventures de Télémaque* was an instant success. Throughout the eighteenth century it was the most widely read book in France and, very possibly, in all of Europe. It was said that, until the publication of Goethe's *The Sorrows of Young Werther,* in 1774, *Télémaque* had no rival in book sales apart from the Bible. It appeared in so many translations that, as one modern scholar has noted, "the exact count of its European translations has yet to be made." It was translated into Latin verse at least twice. The profusion of bilingual editions — Italian-French, German-French — suggests, among other things, that in time Fénelon's text had come to serve as a kind of French-language textbook for foreigners, thereby fulfilling the archbishop's pedagogical aims in ways he cannot have foreseen. Above all, the novel's anti-authoritarian stance and apparent endorsement of universal brotherhood endeared it to the great minds of the Enlightenment. Voltaire praised it as not merely a highly entertaining work of fiction but as a *roman moral;* Montesquieu described it as "the divine book of this century." It was a favorite of other leading lights, from Rousseau (the protagonist of whose own educational-treatise-as-novel, *Émile, or On Education,* happily devours Fénelon's novel) to Thomas Jefferson, the remarkable polymath who was president of the United States of America from 1801 to 1809, an accomplishment he considered less important, if one is to judge from the fact that he neglects to mention it in the epitaph he composed for his funerary monument, than was his founding of the University of Virginia, which he did take care to mention in that memorial text, and which was the institution that I myself attended; that university being founded on the most idealistic pedagogical principles, principles that derived, in part, from Jefferson's devoted reading of *Les aventures de Télémaque,* and which, therefore, I suppose I myself may have absorbed in some small way.

LIKE HOMER'S ODYSSEUS, Fénelon's novel presented different faces to different people. Each era, it seemed, saw in *Télémaque* a reflection of itself. To contemporaries it was a critique of the Sun King: the reading of Louis himself. The Enlightenment philosophers who so admired the book saw in its stalwart anti-authoritarianism, its refreshing emphasis on the happiness of the people, and its assertion of the principle of universal brotherhood, *tous les peuples sont frères, et doivent s'aimer comme tels,* a foreshadowing of their own movement. During the 1780s *Les aventures* was read as a prescient forecast of the Revolution; one pamphlet that circulated at the time was called "Fénelon at the Estates-General." Half a century later — just around the time when the term *Bildungsroman* was coined by the German philologist Karl Morgenstern, a pupil of Friedrich August Wolf, the Homer scholar who founded the modern discipline of philology — the novel's depth of feeling and tender portrayal of the master-student relationship won him new admirers: Stendhal, Sainte-Beuve, Jules Lemaître. At the beginning of the twentieth century, Fénelon and his book were featured in Proust's *In Search of Lost Time,* in which the author of *Les aventures de Télémaque,* along with

Madame de Sévigné and Racine, appears as part of a sacred trio of seventeenth-century authors to whom the narrative often alludes. In the second volume of Proust's immense novel, for instance, the touching character of the grandmother, a great aficionada of Madame de Sévigné in particular, declares that she is full of envy for those who had the privilege of being educated by Fénelon — although it is to be assumed that she is referring in this instance to the duc de Bourgogne and his brothers rather than to Fénelon's students at the Institut des Nouvelles Catholiques, those young girls whose families, buffeted by the tides of politics and religious controversy, had been able to see the handwriting on the wall.

If Fénelon's novel exemplifies one aspect of what I have called the "optimistic" possibilities of narrative — that is, the possibility of infinite digressions within an existing story, of a potentially endless series of smaller concentric circles nested within a larger one; as if Calypso's hollow cave contained a series of smaller hollows — Proust's novel shows us the other optimistic vista. *In Search of Lost Time* suggests that a vast series of digressions could themselves form the largest imaginable ring, one that embraces all of human experience.

The novel famously begins with a description of two digressive possibilities, two "ways" leading to two discrete geographies, each constituting a side, or *côté,* of the Narrator's mental map: the two possible directions in which one could take a walk upon leaving his Aunt Léonie's house in the country town of Combray, where he and his family spent their Easter holidays. When he was young, the

Narrator muses, these two *côtés* seemed to be not merely discrete but opposite to each other:

> For there were, in the environs of Combray, two "ways" which we used to take for our walks, and so diametrically opposed that we would actually leave the house by a different door, according to the way we had chosen: the way towards Méséglise-la-Vineuse, which we called also "Swann's way," because, to get there, one had to pass along the boundary of M. Swann's estate, and the "Guermantes way."

Swann's way, as the Narrator observes, strays past the country home of the Jewish socialite and art collector Charles Swann, a family friend whose obsessive love for the courtesan Odette de Crécy provides a template for the Narrator's later passions, one of which, during his adolescence, will be for the young daughter of Swann and Odette, Gilberte; and the greatest and most obsessive of which, for a young woman called Albertine Simonet, will eventually preoccupy entire volumes of the novel. (One of these is called *The Prisoner,* a title that could well be used for Book 5 of the *Odyssey.*) The Guermantes way, on the other hand, leads to the country seat belonging to the supremely aristocratic family with whose manners, lives, and activities the Narrator is equally obsessed.

As many critics have observed, each of these ways is highly symbolic of a discrete set of themes — themes that, by means of fantastically elaborated series of narrations and digressions, are exhaustively treated in the course of the novel's four thousand pages. Swann's way evokes the world as it is: the strivings of the upper middle classes (one exemplar of which, a character comments, "is a greater liar than Odysseus, the greatest of all liars"), the Dreyfus Affair, politics, diplomacy, international affairs, religion, the demimonde, sex; and also, by association with a series of creative artists whose existences brush against those of Swann and the Narrator and his family, the life of the mind, the world of art, music, and literature. The Guermantes way, by contrast, represents a kind of myth — of aristocratic society, of history, of French national and cultural identity and ideology as represented by a rarefied distillation of that society's manners, clothes, attitudes, and attributes. In the passage about the two ways which I have just quoted, the Narrator refers to this myth as an ideal, although his increasing exposure to the Guermantes and their set begins to erode that ideal, as it becomes clear that this "way" shares many characters, qualities, and attributes with the other "way"—a tantalizing hint that the two ways may be not so much opposite poles on a line than two arcs of the same circle. This possibility is very far from the mind of the Narrator in his childhood, of course, when, as Proust writes, "to 'take the Guermantes way' in order to get to Méséglise, or *vice versa,* would have seemed to me as nonsensical a proceeding as to turn to the east in order to reach the west."

The unexpectedly vast embrace of the novel, the ultimate unity and purposefulness (as the Narrator will perceive following a revelation late in the final volume) of a narrative that so often seems meandering and digressive, is enacted in miniature at various points throughout its seven volumes, as if to reassure the discerning reader that there is in fact a plan at work, even though the totality of that plan will not be perceptible until the final pages of his novel. An excellent example of this phenomenon can be found in the second volume, *À l'ombre des jeunes filles en fleurs*, "Within a Budding Grove," which covers the period of the Narrator's adolescence and awakening sexuality. Beginning in Paris with the young Marcel's immature crush on Gilberte Swann, this installment eventually takes him to the Normandy seaside resort of Balbec, where he is drawn into a circle of vivacious young girls — the "budding young women" to whom the title refers. One of these girls is Albertine, on whom, as a scene toward the end of this volume makes clear, the Narrator decides to settle his affections as the result almost of a whim, a decision whose seemingly arbitrary origins will strike the reader as ironic, given the impact Albertine will have on his life and the huge role that the affair will play in the novel as a whole, serving as a vehicle for its ongoing autopsy of desire, creativity, identity, and time.

How does the affair begin? "Now and then," the Narrator recalls in the second half of *Within a Budding Grove*, "a pretty attention from one or another [of the girls] would stir in me vibrations which dissipated for a time my desire for the rest." One day, he goes on, during a seaside outing with her friends, Albertine writes a message on a piece of paper, which she then hands to the Narrator. The message says, "I like you." Yet the Narrator's response, which will have such seismic repercussions for his whole life, is held at bay until the end of a long scene — a "self-contained whole," as W. A. A. Van Otterlo might have described it in one of his papers of the 1940s — that is triggered by the words "I like you." Precisely like the scene in the *Odyssey* when the nurse Eurycleia recognizes the scar of Odysseus, that dramatic moment which is then frozen while the narrative spins back in time to give us the history of the scar and, beyond that, of Odysseus's name and identity, the critical moment of pregnant recognition toward the end of Proust's second volume is held in abeyance until the narration can circle outward and incorporate some crucial information about the characters before returning to the moment of recognition, which is in fact marked here by a repetition of the words "I like you," and which ultimately illuminates the nature and scope of his own novel, suggesting the enormous range of its themes, techniques, and interests.

Just after the Narrator reads the fateful words, Albertine, as if embarrassed by her note, hastily changes the subject — the subject to which she now addresses herself being, as it happens, the education of young girls. She tells her friends that she has received some mail from their schoolmate Gisèle, who has sent along an exam essay she's just completed in the hope that it might be useful to them in taking their own exams. Albertine fishes out Gisèle's letter and rather officiously begins to summarize it for her friends as they picnic on the Normandy beach: the beginning of a scene that charmingly evokes the adolescent schoolgirls' world, their preoccupations and behavior . . . As once did, in a different context of course, the Polish survivor I'd interviewed in Bondi Beach, who had grinned as he recalled to me how expensive it once had been for my great-uncle to send his four daughters to school (this being an ideal example, as he saw it, of the quotidian, middle-class lives they had all lived before the onset of the Occupation, after which they were being hunted down like animals), and who, despairing of his abilities to convey in words what one of those girls, who during the war would have been about Albertine's age, looked like when she went to school each day, suddenly picked up a sheaf of papers and stuffed them in a satchel and strode around his living room, enacting the winningly energetic ways that that particular lost schoolgirl had once had.

Gisèle, we learn as Albertine reads on, has had to choose between two prompts, both concerning the theater of Racine, that great favorite of the Narrator's grandmother. The choice of playwright in this scene is, indeed, carefully prepared. Earlier on, before the action moves to Balbec, we learn a great deal about the Narrator's obsessive interest in a great actress called Berma and her acclaimed performances in Racine's *Phèdre*—a work, based on Euripides's *Hippolytus,* whose theme of one-sided erotic obsession underscores the motif of anguished, unrequited passion that courses through Proust's novel. But the plays about which Gisèle's teacher has asked are not Racine's well-known works inspired by classical antiquity; they are, rather, based on incidents from the Old Testament and Jewish history. The first prompt is, "Sophocles, from the Shades, writes to Racine to console him for the failure of *Athalie*"; the second, "Suppose that, after the first performance of *Esther,* Mme de Sévigné is writing to Mme de la Fayette to tell her how much she regretted her absence." Now *Esther* (1689) is a dramatization of the story from the Book of Esther about the triumph of the eponymous Jewish queen over her enemy, the evil Persian grand vizier Haman (in French, *Aman*), who had planned to wipe out the Jewish people. *Athalie* (1691), Racine's final work for the stage, is about how a virtuous priest of the Temple in Jerusalem triumphs over an evil queen — the ruthless Athaliah, who forsakes the worship of the one true god and shows herself willing to murder even guiltless babes in her mad quest for power. These allusions to Jewish suffering evoked in Proust's choice of subjects for the girls' test questions are not incidental to *À la recherche,* much of which is preoccupied with Jews and their place in French society, from Charles Swann in the first volume to the Dreyfus Affair, by which French society was riven and which becomes central to later installments.

Gisèle had chosen to reply to the first prompt, which requires her to impersonate Sophocles as he writes from the dead to the crestfallen Racine following the debacle of *Athalie*'s premiere. (The play's failure, according to the nineteenth-century French critic Gustave Merlet, stemmed in part from the drab simplicity of the cheap sets, which could not come close to reproducing the magnificence of Solomon's Temple.) Gisèle begins by having Sophocles congratulate Racine for managing to create a moving tragedy in which religious piety, rather than erotic passion, is the "keynote"—for writing a play that (to put it another way) follows the Hebrew rather than the Greek paradigm. Her Sophocles then admires Racine for giving great poetry not only to the various characters but to the chorus: "a veritable novelty in France." If the play's moral loftiness and artistic innovations failed to impress the public at its premiere, this fictional Sophocles concludes, it was the fault of the public's, rather than the author's, taste.

Albertine is deeply impressed by her friend's cleverness. But when she finishes reading Gisèle's letter — the letter, we remember, that is keeping the Narrator in anguished suspense about the love-note he received only minutes before — another member of the little band of girls, Andrée, chimes in with a devastating critique of Gisèle's exam paper, creating a second ring within the digression initiated by Albertine's reading and, not incidentally, manufacturing still more agonizing suspense for the Narrator.

Andrée begins by deriding Gisèle's paper as meandering and disordered. How much better to begin with an outline or rough sketch! For in that way, with a summary to refer to, "you know where you are." Point by point, she then demolishes her friend's arguments, dismissing the praise of *Athalie*'s pious subject matter as woefully ahistorical (the Hebrew and Greek religions were too different for useful comparison, she declares), and deriding the idea that Racine's lyrical choruses were an innovation (she rattles off examples of much earlier plays — one about Haman and Esther, another about Nebuchadnezzar and his persecution of the Jews — that gave beautiful verse to the chorus). As for placing the blame for the failure of *Athalie* on the public's poor taste, Andrée reminds the girls that it was "not for the general public but before the Sun King and a few privileged courtiers that *Athalie* was first played" —

among which privileged courtiers, as Proust, that lover of
seventeenth-century literature and court gossip, must have
known, was François Fénelon, invited to join the king's
circle as a tribute to his pedagogical services to the royal
family. Andrée ends her diatribe by airily recommending
that her friends acquaint themselves with the work of the
critic Gustave Merlet.

It is at this moment — the moment that confirms Albertine's inferior intellectual panache and expertise, in comparison to those of Andrée — that Proust's digression ends
and the narrative returns to the urgent present, a return
signaled by the repetition of the words "I like you":

> Meanwhile, I had been thinking of the little page torn
> from a scribbling block which Albertine had handed
> me. "I like you," she had written. And an hour later . . .
> I said to myself that it was with her that I would have
> my romance.

And so the digression that begins with that scribbled
"I like you" and then veers violently away from the quotidian world of adolescent girlish worries, the crushes and
the school examinations, to a series of references first to
the large outside world and its concerns — royalty, politics,
intolerance, war, religion; and thence to the rarefied fields
of literature, theater, stage design, art, criticism, history —
the digression that begins and ends with the childishly
simple "I like you," which we know will be a harbinger of
the most excruciating adult emotions imaginable, has in
fact ended up traveling down the two "ways" introduced in
Proust's first volume: the two vast and seemingly discrete

geographies which so surprisingly come together to constitute the world itself.

So too, as we learn at the end of Proust's novel, do the two roads which (the Narrator had thought in his childhood) went in opposite directions from his great-aunt's house in Combray turn out, in reality, to be one and the same. In the opening pages of the final volume, *Le temps retrouvé,* "Time Regained," the Narrator returns as an adult to Combray and there visits his childhood love, Gilberte, who is by now a grown woman trapped in an unhappy marriage. Gilberte surprises the Narrator in a number of ways during their conversations, not least on the occasion when, in the course of one of their pleasant walks around the old town, Gilberte makes a startling suggestion:

> Gilberte said to me: "If you like, we might after all go out one afternoon and then we can go to Guermantes, taking the road by Méséglise ['Swann's way'], which is the nicest way," a sentence which upset all the ideas of my childhood by informing me that the two "ways" were not as irreconcilable as I had supposed.

The two routes radiating out from his family home, the Narrator and the reader of the novel now learn, are not vectors but rather arcs of a circle, components of a ring that circumnavigates the town.

That this insight marks the beginning of the final volume is no accident. Here, just as at the end of the *Odyssey,* a series of climactic recognitions signals the gigantic coherence of the work itself. Some of those recognitions are ironic, even bitter. There is, for instance, the information, revealed to the Narrator by Gilberte during one of their chats, that she had been as attracted to him in their youth as he had been to her. As intensely as he'd been studying her, it turns out, he had been blind to the signal that (as she can now admit) she had been trying to send one day when he passed by Swann's house and had caught sight of her, a scene described in the novel's first volume, *Swann's Way.* The meaning of the vulgar gesture she had made as he passed by, which had seemed obvious to her, was nonetheless misinterpreted at the time by the Narrator — a mistake, he now realizes, that had determined the course of his entire life. This climactic insight suggests that even the most ardent intellects, the greatest minds, can fail at interpretation, can fail to "read" the world correctly, until it is too late.

The unity of the two ways, Swann's and the Guermantes', has in fact already been hinted at by this point in *À la recherche,* symbolized by a marriage between a Swann and a Guermantes: the union of Gilberte herself, the daughter of Charles Swann, to a beloved friend of the Narrator who belongs, ostensibly, to the "Guermantes way" — a young man called Robert de Saint-Loup, a nephew of the duc and duchesse de Guermantes. The choice of groom is important. More than most characters in Proust, Saint-Loup himself is riven by extraordinary oppositions — as his strange and striking name, whose literal meaning is "Saint-Wolf," seems to hint — combining within himself many opposite "ways." A sensitive intellectual and a tradition-bound officer, an aristocrat and a liberal, heterosexual and homosexual, Robert is an enigma who never stops fascinating the Narrator, from his first appearance in *Within a Budding Grove* to his heroic death at the German front during World War I, referred to in *Time Regained.*

In the final pages of *À l'ombre des jeunes filles en fleurs,* the author reminds us that we must be on guard against the impulse to locate the reality behind our fictions, since reality is usually so much more dreary. "Geographers or archaeologists may conduct us over Calypso's island, may excavate the Palace of Minos. Only, Calypso becomes then a mere woman, Minos a mere king . . ." Still, many of the characters and locales we encounter in his novel were based on real people and places, and it is almost impossible to resist the temptation to trace the resemblances between the fictional and the real. We know, for instance, that Saint-Loup was based on a real person. Around the turn of the twentieth century the author had made the acquaintance of a handsome young aristocrat called Bertrand, a diplomat who was posted at one point to the faraway Ottoman capital: a frustration about which Proust complains bitterly in his letters to his friend Antoine Bibesco. But if the thought of Constantinople (as Proust calls Istanbul in his letters) tormented the writer, there was another locale associated with his dashing young friend for which the author could only be grateful. Bertrand was descended from a great family that had thrown off several prominent Catholic prelates, one of whom presided over a see — the very place, in fact, where Proust in his novel locates the front where Saint-Loup is killed — called Cambrai. There can be little doubt that this place, long associated with Bertrand's family, inspired the fictional name "Combray" in Proust's novel:

the town, with its highly symbolic geographies, where the Narrator encounters the two ways which at first he believed were distinct but turn out to be one.

In a letter to Bibesco dated August 1910, a dejected Proust, recognizing that Bertrand, who was then heading off again to the distant Ottoman capital, was yet another in a long series of loves as unrequited as Phèdre's, charmingly evokes his friend's appealing ways and good looks. Of particular beauty, Proust writes, were Bertrand's eyes, his *yeux blu de mer qui viennent en droite ligne de Télémaque et de l'île de Calypso,* his sea-blue eyes that come straight from Telemachus and the island of Calypso. The compliment would not have surprised those who, like the future author of *À la recherche,* had a deep intimacy with the history of the French nobility. For it happens that striking eyes were a noted feature of Bertrand's family going back several centuries. In the 1680s, for example, Saint-Simon described one of Bertrand's distant relations as having eyes "whose fire and wit sprang forth like a torrent." Reading his words, I find it impossible not to think of Auerbach's *gemeinsame Verbindung,* that deep connectedness among things which, for the optimist at least, is sometimes detectable in history as well as in literature. The flashing-eyed relative in question was François-Armand de Salignac de La Mothe-Fénelon, author of *Les aventures de Télémaque,* tutor to Louis XIV's grandson, and archbishop of Cambrai.

3

THE TEMPLE

[Πόλις] Sola Constantinopolis a Graecis hodie appellatur per excellentiam, cum urbes caeteras omnes κάστρα vocare soleant. Unde accidit ut ex στὴν πόλιν quomodo vulgus dicere amabat, cum Byzantium proficiscebantur, aut de hac urbe loquebantur, Turci fecerunt . . . Στάμβουλ

Today only Constantinople is called *Polis* [the City] by the Greeks, due to its preëminence; they refer to all other cities as *kastra*. Whence it came about that, from *stin polin* [to the City], which is how ordinary people liked to refer to the city whenever they would set out for Byzantium or speak about it, the Turks made the name *Stamboul* . . .

> —Du Cange, *Glossarium ad scriptores mediae et infimae*
> *Graecitatis* (1687), on the derivation of the name
> Stamboul [Istanbul]

Der oriental. (-türk.) name *Stambul* ist eine verstümmelung von *islam* = rechtglaübig und *bul* = menge oder vielheit.

The Oriental (-Turkish) name *Stamboul* is a corruption of *Islam* = "true belief" and *bul* = "a mass or abundance."

> —Johann Jacob Egli, *Nomina geographica* (1872)

A STRANGER REACHES an unknown city after a long voyage. The journey has been winding and full of complications; the stranger is tired. He approaches at last the building that will be his home from now on and, perhaps with a little sigh, begins walking toward it, the final short length of the improbably meandering way that has led him here. Perhaps there are stairs. If so, he mounts them wearily. Or maybe there is an arch through which he vanishes, a small smudge against the gaping darkness, like some character in a myth disappearing into the jaws of a monster. His shoulders are likely hunched by the weight of the bags he is carrying, the two bags which now are everything he has, apart from the wife and the child. When are they coming? The bags were packed in haste: what to take, what is most precious? One of them likely contains books.

Who is he? He is the Greek scholar fleeing Istanbul for Italy in 1453, the Muslim fled from Spain to Istanbul in 1492, the Huguenot running from France to Germany in 1685, the Jew fleeing Germany early in the last century, as so many did, as Erich Auerbach did, for instance, in 1936, when he ran from Marburg to, of all places, Istanbul, whose university offered him a refuge, that ornate house with its ravishing views of the sea where he wrote *Mimesis,* his hymn to the greatness of European civilization. Or he is a writer seventy years later who for a while was plunged into helpless despair, *aporia,* after he spent years researching a book that describes the effects of the cataclysm that swept up Auerbach and, among millions of others, a handful of people living in a small Polish town, some of whom, like the German scholar, tried to escape, although their escape was not successful; a writer who now warily contemplates a new book, a book about a marvelous and charming poem, the *Odyssey* (which for a brief period he studied with his father, an illuminating experience), a poem which, as we know, once interested Auerbach, too; warily contemplates a book about this great masterpiece which, the despairing writer hopes, will spare him having to tell any more of the terrible stories he once had to tell.

Or maybe he is another kind of writer, one who wants to get away not from the tales of horrors suffered by the victims but from the inherited guilt for those horrors—from a past for which he is not responsible but by which he feels tainted. Maybe he is Winfried Georg Maximilian Sebald, born in the Gau, the Nazi administrative district of Schwaben, in Bavaria, in 1944 and therefore, as it were, a guiltless babe when the atrocities that had pushed Auerbach to Istanbul were still taking place; a German who nonetheless felt compelled to leave his country in the 1960s, indeed to leave behind his own father, a man who throughout the Second World War had fought in the Wehrmacht, a division whose motto was *Gott mit uns,* God with Us. Compelled, then, to leave his native land not by a royal edict but by his own sense of claustrophobic shame, this German writer comes to the country of those who defeated his own and finds himself, in time, standing before the door of the Department of European Literature of the University of East Anglia, where he will spend the rest of his too-short life writing books about exiles, émigrés. About *Ausgewanderten,* to use the German word, which will indeed be the title of one of his books: emigrants, people who have been forced to "wander outward" into the world just as, all those centuries ago, Odysseus was sent reeling through space and time, *mala pollà plangthê,* cast off, set adrift, baffled, balked. In photographs taken of Sebald in his middle age, self-exile seems to have smoothed him out: the plump oval face, with its shock of white hair receding from the expansive brow, strikes you as both intelligent and quizzical, even comic, the straight graying eyebrows shooting up at a forty-five-degree angle as if in amusement at some joke you have arrived too late to hear, the dark eyes hooded by the skin of the lids, which droop like curtains across the outer corners, obscuring most of the whites and leaving only the large dark irises visible. These are, you cannot help feeling, the eyes of someone prone to melancholy.

Let us leave them there for now, the two Germans, Auerbach in Istanbul safely ensconced with his chair in Western Languages and Literatures and his tortured dream of *die gemeinsame Verbindung der Kulturen,* Sebald standing before the door of the Department of European Literature in East Anglia, wondering what awaits him, as so many millions of others through the millennia have stood and wondered before strange gateways and buildings and doors, flung across the globe to these once unimaginable locations, these unlikely places of refuge from the people, or merely the memories, that are hunting them.

IT IS NOT DIFFICULT to understand Erich Auerbach's distrust of ring composition and the sense it can give you

that there is a profound, almost supernatural connectedness between events. If the refugee German Jew found
Homer's all-illuminating device to be inconsistent with
the inscrutable mechanics of real life, if he preferred the
inexplicable omissions and gaps that characterize the narrative style of the Hebrew Bible, a style that refuses to reveal, as ring composition insists on doing, connections between things, inside and outside, motivations and actions,
past and present, well, who could blame him? Who could
question his attraction to the opaque, pessimistic narrative
mode, given the awful circumstances in which he wrote
Mimesis, the harrowing flight to his improbable Asian refuge from a Europe in which the only remaining connectedness among cultures was a negative one: the common
experience of annihilation?

   Auerbach's distrust of the Greek technique raises a larger
question about the problems of representation in literature,
about the means by which writers make their subjects seem
"realistic." Naturally this question has plagued all kinds of
artists as they have struggled with difficult subjects, one of
the greatest and most difficult of these being, in our own
time, the event that landed Auerbach in Istanbul: the German plan to exterminate the Jews of Europe during World
War II. The difficulty of representation posed by this unimaginably destructive event was most famously, if contro-
versially, expressed in the oft-quoted dictum of Auerbach's
fellow German refugee Theodor Adorno: *nach Auschwitz
ein Gedicht zu schreiben, ist barbarisch,* "to write a poem
after Auschwitz is barbaric." But the problem has plagued
all kinds of writers with regard to all kinds of subjects.

Sometimes when this subject comes up, for instance, I find myself thinking of the curious story of the failure, when it was first presented in 1691, of Racine's final tragedy, *Athalie*. As we know, *Athalie* together with its immediate predecessor, *Esther,* represented a startling departure in the work of Racine, whose earlier plays had been inspired by Greek or Roman themes. For this abandonment of pagan in favor of biblical subjects there was a compelling and, perhaps, not wholly artistic reason. These two final plays were written to please Mme. de Maintenon, the fiercely pious morganatic wife of Louis XIV; both were first performed at Saint-Cyr, the girls' school of which she was the patron — the education of young Catholic girls being, as we know, a subject of urgent importance in the final decades of the seventeenth century in France, as witness the career of François Fénelon, head of the Institut des Nouvelles Catholiques. And indeed we are told that Racine, in being commissioned to write something for the girls of Saint-Cyr, was urged to turn away from classical literature and find inspiration in a Hebrew text in part because Mme. de Maintenon had become alarmed by the unseemly passions evident in the girls' earlier performance of Racine's *Andromaque:* a work based on Euripides's play about the widow of the Trojan hero Hector, a woman who, according to the Greek myth, had been unable to hide her small son successfully from the Greeks who were hunting him as they sacked Troy and who, when they found the child, tossed him from the top of the city's wall. Mme. de Maintenon had been alarmed, too, by the excessive vanity and preening to which *Andromaque*'s success had moved some of the girls, those qualities being inimical to the Catholic values Louis's secret wife sought to instill in her students. I find myself enjoying this latter anecdote, which carries over the centuries such an unexpectedly distinct flavor of those lost schoolgirls and their ways: the vanity and silliness, the seriousness and yearnings, all of which can be so hard to imagine, to re-create.

So you might say that, as his career moved toward its end, Racine's oeuvre came to exemplify the dual inheritance of European culture, the Greco-Roman and the Judeo-Christian, that has twined its way through the work of European thinkers as different as Johann Reuchlin in the fifteenth century, that Renaissance humanist who insisted that knowledge of Hebrew be paired with that of Greek and Latin in German education, and who happened to be a student of Jan Lascaris, one of the hundreds of Byzantine scholars displaced by the Fall of Constantinople in 1453; and Erich Auerbach in the twentieth, who begins his masterpiece *Mimesis* by contrasting the Homeric and the biblical styles of narration.

Racine's *Esther* was a great success, but as the schoolgirls in Proust's novel knew, the premiere of *Athalie* was a failure. The play depicts the downfall of the murderous ninth-century BC Jewish queen Athaliah, a daughter of Ahab and Jezebel who, in her lust for power, ordered the murders of all potential claimants to the throne, including the children of her own line, unaware that one child had been safely hidden away — the one who, in time, would finally supplant her. To those who find this harrowing play, the climax of which is set inside the Great Temple of

Solomon itself, to be Racine's finest, the story of its failure
seems inexplicable. But fail it did. As I have mentioned,
Gustave Merlet, the nineteenth-century critic, attributed
the *débacle* to the drab simplicity of the production values,
which, no doubt in keeping with Mme. de Maintenon's
renewed desire to instill modesty in her students, were required to be as simple as possible, in stark contrast to the
lavish sets and costumes that were to be seen in *Esther* two
years earlier. Those who disdained the production com-
plained in particular of the failure of Racine's *mise-en-scène*
to reproduce the magnificence of the Temple, which, in
the Saint-Cyr production, was merely suggested by some
lavish swags that in any case were hard to see. *Son temple
n'a que des festons magnifiques, et encore on ne les voit pas . . .*
All this concern over the accuracy of the representation of
the Temple, it should be said, will strike some people as
ironic. Its magnificence, after all, is something we can only
imagine. For the Temple was destroyed not once but twice.
Solomon's grandiose building was leveled to the ground
by the Babylonian king Nebuchadnezzar in 587 BC during
his conquest of the Jewish state of Judah, the defeat that
resulted in the exile of the Jews to Babylon, the Babylonian
Captivity; and, in a nightmarish repetition, the replacement for that Temple which the Jews subsequently built,
the so-called Second Temple, was sacked, looted, and razed
in AD 70 by the Romans during the First Jewish War. Of
that second structure, only part of a wall remains, that one
fragment occupying a site that has since become an object
of sometimes violent controversy, it being sacred at once to
Jews and Muslims.

The difficulty of representing the past accurately — even if that past is itself a dream, a reconstruction of a reconstruction, a palimpsest of a palimpsest — is one known to people other than writers, of course. I have mentioned that I was a fervent model-maker in my early teenage years, often devoting all of my after-school time to making intricate reproductions of buildings from antiquity. Of these, the Parthenon was the object of an almost obsessive interest. After making my first model of it for a class project when I was about twelve, using cardboard toilet paper rolls to stand in for the original's elegantly fluted Doric columns, I embarked on creating a proper scale model, three feet wide by six feet long, the ambitiousness of which now strikes me as almost absurd and the construction of which was never completed although it absorbed the next five years of my life. During that period my skills improved. I studied dozens of books and, eventually, created elaborate rubber molds from which I could cast the forty-six columns of the peristyle and other architectural elements. I reproduced as meticulously as I was able the bas-reliefs of the frieze, which I worked in Plasticine on one-inch-high strips of cardboard, and the great chryselephantine statue of Athena, which in my three-feet-to-an-inch scale rendering was thirteen inches high, cast in plaster, and adorned with real gold leaf. Given how intense my focus on this project was, it's odd that I now neither know nor care what became of the elements that I had finished. Or perhaps not odd, since later in my adolescence the desire to build my model suddenly evaporated. All at once, it seemed, the effort required to finish casting the columns was impossibly daunting, although the casting process, which was quite simple compared to the research and the artisanal processes required to create the molds, was by then the only thing that stood between me and completion. After years of fervent daily activity, the entire project was beginning to seem pointless; now, as I entered my high school years, it was enough for me to descend every few days into the cellar and survey the disassembled pieces that were neatly lined up or stacked on the large worktable, the columns, the architrave, the pediments with their heavy ornamentation, the gaudy cult statue gleaming even in the darkness of the slightly damp underground space. It was as if, having imagined the model for so long, having so minutely researched the structure and pored over all the books and plans, the vision of it that I had for so long had in my head was sufficient; I knew what it should look like, I knew where each piece, down to the tiniest *gutta,* needed to be positioned. And so the model itself now struck me as an afterthought. By this point I was seventeen or eighteen and the interests that had sustained me through a solitary puberty, particularly classical archaeology, with its exciting promise of great riches lurking just below the surface, had yielded to a keen interest in literature. I began to keep a diary; I started to write stories and poems. Now, too, I wanted to learn Greek; the books that I took out of the library each week were volumes of Sophocles and Plato's *Phaedrus,* works that left me with inchoate and exalted yearnings that no model could ever depict. And indeed not long after this period of my life I went off to university to study Greek literature, which, however much it has suffered at the hands of time, has only rarely been the object of the kind of intentional ruination that has left such scant traces of so many ancient structures.

One of the best examples of such deliberate destruction is the Parthenon itself. In a curious coincidence, the building to which I once had devoted so much thought and energy was — like the Second Temple of Jerusalem — built to replace an earlier temple that had been destroyed. That earlier temple to Athena, goddess of wisdom and patroness of Athens (and, too, of Odysseus) had been set afire and razed to the ground by the Persian King Darius when he invaded Athens in 490 BC, fresh from his conquests in Babylon. The building we know today, constructed between 447 and 432 BC as a replacement for that earlier ruin, eventually became one of the most iconic works of architecture in the world. Or, I should say, one of the most iconic ruins. For the Parthenon had remained more or less intact, had looked more or less as it had looked when it was completed in 432, until the 26th of September 1687, when, as part of an action during the so-called Great Turkish War between the Venetians and the Ottomans — the war in which Fénelon's brother had distinguished himself — a Venetian commander named Morosoni, having been informed that the Turks were using the former Greek temple as a powder magazine (information given to him on the — as it turned out — naïve assumption that it would stop him targeting the structure), fired on the building. The resultant explosion destroyed almost all of its interior structures, much of its peristyle, and many of its lavish sculptures. The human cost included the horrible deaths of more than

three hundred Muslims who had taken shelter in this one-
time temple to Athena — a troubling irony, given that we
owe a good deal of what we know about the Parthenon's
appearance before the explosion to the descriptions in the
travel writings of a Muslim, the celebrated Turkish diarist
Evliya Çelebi.

One result of the physical devastation suffered by
the building in 1687 was that, almost from the moment
Greece won its independence from its Ottoman overlords
at the beginning of the nineteenth century, the Parthenon has been the object of almost continual attempts at
restoration — although the word "restoration" raises per-
plexing questions about memory and history, since the
building that began as a temple to a pagan goddess had
many subsequent religious and architectural incarnations
in its long history, for instance as a mosque, complete with
a minaret, although those subsequent incarnations were
not the object of any restorative energies, it having been
decided that the single moment in this building's past that
ought to be preserved was the earliest, Periclean one, the
one that corresponded to the cultural identity that the
newly independent Greek state of the 1820s wanted to cling
to: that of a free and powerful Hellenic people cleansed,
as it were, of the encrustations of later history, just as the
Acropolis and the Parthenon itself would be cleansed of
the traces of that later history. Although it is tempting to
decry the Greeks' decision to restore only those bits of their
monuments that corresponded to their present ideological
needs, I for one have a certain sympathy for it. Were someone to raise enough money to restore the Great Synagogue

of Bolechów, after all, would we not want it to appear as it did in, say, 1908, the year my great-uncle had his bar mitzvah there — would we not want it to look as it looked when the culture that produced that particular structure was at its height, just as the Athens that produced the Parthenon was a culture at its height? 1908, which is to say three decades before that same great-uncle was hunted to his death in that same small town after hiding for some time in a dark and secret place, like a small animal: one among many people who failed to hide successfully and who, on being found, were shot on the spot or transported to camps or, in the cases of certain children I have heard about, tossed to their deaths from the upper stories of the Town Hall. These were the people whose disappearance would lead, in time, to the decay of the Great Synagogue, that once-impressive structure, to the loss of memory of what the building was and how it was supposed to function and look, with the inevitable result that it would, in time, be encrusted with additions (those Ukrainian folkart murals of rural landscapes, for instance) that our restorative efforts would be meant to purge. Such is the hold that these buildings, or rather the identities that they represent, have on the imagination — of entire nations as well as of individual enthusiasts.

Anyway, that odd youthful pastime of mine is no doubt why I was so strongly affected by a certain passage toward the end of a novel called *The Rings of Saturn,* originally published in 1995 as *Die Ringe des Saturn,* by the late W. G. Sebald, the German writer who had emigrated in the 1960s to the United Kingdom, where he spent the rest of his life and which is the setting for much of his writing. It was in England, oddly enough, that Sebald wrote his dissertation on the German writer Alfred Döblin, author of the masterwork *Berlin Alexanderplatz* and himself a Jewish refugee from Hitler, just as Auerbach was. (Döblin and Auerbach, in fact, died within weeks of each other, in 1957: the kind of near-coincidence beloved of Sebald, as we shall see.) Small wonder that, as has been observed by many critics by now, emigration, wandering, flight, and exile are the hallmarks of Sebald's strange novels. *Vertigo* (1990) features dream-like Alpine travelogues narrated by a neurotically unhappy figure who could or could not be the author himself ("what else could I do . . . but wander aimlessly around until well into the night?"), as well as vignettes from the lives of those great travelers Casanova and Stendhal, the latter of whom is plagued, in Sebald's narration of the Frenchman's trip to the site of the Battle of Marengo, by anxieties about how we represent the past, anxieties that in fact explain the title of the novel. "The difference between the images of the battle which he had in his head," Sebald writes of Stendhal, "and what he now saw before him . . . occasioned in him a vertiginous sense of confusion such as he had never previously experienced." *The Emigrants* (1992) consists of four long narratives about men, some German, some Jewish, and finally including the author himself, whose worldwide wanderings are all ultimately revealed to be deeply connected to the tragic history of Germany in the twentieth century. *The Rings of Saturn,* which was published in 1995, I shall describe presently. As for Sebald's final novel — the author died in a car accident in 2001, at the age of fifty-seven—it is called *Austerlitz:* a reference of course to another great Napoleonic battle, but here the name of the title character, yet another *Ausgewanderter,* who, we learn, had come to England as a child in a *Kindertransport* and whose adult journeys in search of information about the fate of his mother structure the novel's action—if we may refer to the movement of a narrative that is so diffuse, so meandering, so ruminative, as "action."

Given my own history with such journeys in search of the Holocaust past, it would seem natural for *Austerlitz* to be my favorite of Sebald's novels. And indeed, toward the climax of that fictional tale it is revealed that, during the wandering that he undertakes in search of his origins, Austerlitz has been carrying with him a copy of a book called *Heshel's Kingdom,* a real work by the South African writer Dan Jacobson which has much in common with the one that I would later write. *Heshel's Kingdom* traces its author's travels through Lithuania during the 1990s, where he had set out in search of traces of his grandfather Heshel's lost world, a world very much like the one my relatives in Bolechów inhabited. This real-life memoir, which Sebald's fictional character carries everywhere with him, is, like my own book, an example of a now-flourishing genre of narratives about emotionally fraught Jewish returns to the irretrievably lost "old country" (as Jewish émigrés of my own grandfather's generation called Eastern Europe); still, I could not have predicted that I would end up writing such a book back in the early 1990s, when I was in graduate school writing a dissertation about Greek tragedy and one of my closest friends was Dan Jacobson's nephew, David, who spoke often of his uncle and his work . . . *Austerlitz* is to some extent anomalous among Sebald's novels precisely because of its explicit mention of the German extermination of the Jews of Europe, which haunts his other narratives without ever quite being made explicit. To my knowledge there is only one time in Sebald's work that the word "Holocaust" occurs, and there it refers not to what Germany did to the Jews but to what, in the Book of Genesis, Abraham intends to do to Isaac. In a typically digressive passage in *The Rings of Saturn,* which indeed consists of nothing but digressions, a series of tales that both describe and mirror its narrator's meandering walks around the East Coast of England during a period of inexplicable depression, the narrator muses on the 1658 work by Thomas Browne called *Hydriotaphia, or Urn-Burial,* whose discussion of how easy it is to burn human bodies is paraphrased at one point:

> it is not difficult to burn a human body: a piece of an old boat burnt Pompey, and the King of Castile burnt large numbers of Saracens with next to no fuel, the fire being visible far and wide. Indeed . . . if the burthen of Isaac were sufficient for an holocaust, a man may carry his own pyre.

The scene to which Thomas Browne here refers is the one which, in *Mimesis,* Erich Auerbach uses as an exemplum of the opaque Hebraic style.

As I have implied, *The Rings of Saturn* is the most emblematic of this author's strange style, which is why it is in fact my favorite of his novels; that style being characterized by frequent recourse to the technique hinted at by his title's reference to rings. Like Homer, Sebald uses ring composition to great effect. But unlike the narrative rings, circles, digressions, and wandering that we find in Homer, which seem designed both to illuminate and to enact a hidden unity in things, the ones we find in Sebald seem designed to confuse, entangling his characters in meanderings from which they cannot extricate themselves and which have no clear destination. In *The Rings of Saturn,* the meticulously traced trajectories of both history and nature lead only to dissolution and defeat. In the opening pages of the novel we are told that the narrator's penchant for those long wandering walks around the countryside bring him repeatedly in contact with what he calls "traces of destruction"— whether of the people of the Congo, whose oppression at the hands of Belgian capitalists is the subject of one of the book's most harrowing excurses, obliquely inspired by one such walk; or of the Dutch elm tree, the devastation of which by a virus in England in the 1980s is described in another lengthy digression. These "traces of destruction" produce in the book's narrator what he calls "a paralyzing horror"—a feeling with which I myself became acquainted after finishing my Holocaust book. The narrator's subsequent encounters, unlike the surprise meetings and reunions in Homer, are never happy ones. A pleasant walk on the grounds of a deserted country estate leads to a conversation with an old caretaker who begins recalling the British bombings of Germany, the sixty-seven airfields in East Anglia, the billion gallons of fuel that propelled the planes that dropped seven hundred and thirty-two thousand tons of bombs on Germany, the nine thousand aircraft lost with their fifty thousand men. A friendly visit to the country home of Sebald's real-life friend Michael Hamburger is also inexorably overshadowed by this awful theme, since much of that visit is taken up first by the German Sebald's guilty thoughts about Hamburger's escape from Berlin as a child — for he was yet another Jewish refugee from Hitler — and, later, by Hamburger's own melancholy reflections on his lost past.

As you make your way through his twisting narratives, it becomes ever more difficult to escape the impression that the circling merely exhausts us while never bringing us any closer to the subject. Whereas Homer's rings whirl us toward revelation and illumination, spinning ever further into Odysseus's past and bringing us to the very moments of his birth and naming, the keys to his and his epic's identity, the circles in Sebald's restless narration lead us to a series of locked doors to which there is no key. The individual stories are often introduced by disquieting near-coincidences — the fact, for instance, that the birthday of Hölderlin's translator should fall a few days *after* that of the poet himself — such noncoincidence reflecting the aura of missed opportunities and failed connections that haunts Sebald's work. Like Proust's digressions and "ways," Sebald's meanderings ultimately form a giant ring that ties together many disparate tales and experiences; but if Proust's ring appears to us as a container, filled with all of human experience, Sebald's embraces a void: a destination to which, as in some narrative version of Zeno's paradox, no amount of writing can deliver us.

The theme of the failure of narrative in fact shadows *The Rings of Saturn* from its opening pages, where a typically odd chain of connections allows the author to introduce this motif. In those pages the narrator describes his walking tours in Suffolk during the dog days of 1992, these tours putting him in mind of a great friend of his who also enjoyed walking tours; but the friend who enjoyed walking, the narrator tells us, died suddenly, a death that particularly affected a certain colleague of the dead man — a woman professor whose work focused on the nineteenth-century novel. This academic specialty inevitably recalls to the narrator's mind the novelist Flaubert, in whom, he observes (paraphrasing the woman professor), "Fear of the false sometimes kept him [Flaubert] confined to his couch for weeks or months on end in the dread that he would never be able to write another word without compromising himself in the most grievous of ways." And yet even this statement of failure is subject to failure, since after all how can we claim to know about Flaubert's crises when (as the narrator also says, this time quoting Diderot), "Who can say how things were in the past?"

The irretrievability of the past turns out to be the main subject of the long conversation that takes place during the narrator's visit to his friend Michael Hamburger. Hamburger describes to him how, many years after the war, he had returned to Berlin and gone to the building where his parents had had their apartment, a building where the plasterwork garlands, the familiar railing, the names on the mailboxes — many of which, Hamburger notes, have not changed — now appear to him like pictures in a rebus that I simply had to puzzle out correctly in order to cancel the monstrous events that had happened since we emigrated. It was as if it were now up to me alone, as if by some trifling mental exertion I could reverse the entire course of history, as if—if I desired it only—Grandmother Antonina, who had refused to go with us to England, would still be living in Kantstraße as before. . . . All that was required was a moment of concentration, piecing together the syllables of the word concealed in the riddle, and everything would again be as it once was. But I could neither make out the word nor bring myself to mount the stairs and ring the bell of our old flat. Instead I left the building with a sick feeling . . .

His inability either to read or to move seems to sum up Sebald's project, in which language fails and motion is pointless. *Everything is left in obscurity.*

THE FUTILITY OF HAMBURGER'S attempts to reach back to the past, let alone reconstruct it, let alone restore what has been destroyed by time or other forces—of attempts even by this master of language, a distinguished poet and literary figure—is the subject of another tale that Sebald tells in *The Rings of Saturn,* forming one of the final narrative rings that make up the novel. This tale is in fact the very one that, as I mentioned earlier, evokes such powerful emotions in me, one of those emotions being a feeling of nostalgic recognition, since the story in question is about an obsessive model-maker.

The narrator's encounter with this figure takes place immediately after a rather allusive episode: his brief visit to a dilapidated estate belonging to some Anglo-Irish aristocrats who had fled Ireland during the Troubles and who are now, like so many of this book's characters, stranded by history. The inertia of their lives is symbolized by the fruitless work done day after day by the daughters of the family, who make marvelous pillowcases and counterpanes by sewing together bits of fabulous old fabrics that they find around the house, only to undo the stitches later, disintegrating their own creations. This story bears an unmistakable resemblance to a tale from Book 2 of the *Odyssey* about Odysseus's wife, Penelope, who promises the Suitors that she will marry one of them as soon as she finishes weaving a shroud for her aged father-in-law but, in order to prolong her capitulation for as long as possible, secretly undoes each day's weaving by night. Because weaving often figures in Greek literature as a symbol for storytelling, for "plotting" (in both senses of that word), it is possible to take the story of Penelope's tactic as a dark parable about a kind of narrative barely imaginable in the epic: about the disquieting possibility that there are stories that can have no ending, that merely spin on pointlessly, as indeed the lives of those Anglo-Irish girls go on with no hope of closure, of narrative satisfaction. It is as if there, at the beginning of the *Odyssey,* Homer were dreaming of Sebald . . .

From this house of mythic stasis the narrator of *The Rings of Saturn* moves on, traveling next to see an old acquaintance of his called Thomas Abrams, a farmer, a pastor, and, we learn, an avid amateur modeler. Abrams, the narrator recalls, had begun his hobbying career by making replicas of ships and other vessels. But by the time Sebald's novel takes place he has spent the past twenty years working obsessively on one model, a model of a single building that, when you consider its maker's résumé, is a most likely subject.

What Abrams is working on is a reproduction of the Temple of Jerusalem. The vast model, which covers ten square yards, seeks to re-create everything, the "antechambers and the living quarters of the priesthood, the Roman garrison, the bath-houses, the market stalls, the sacrificial altars, covered walkways and the booths of the money-lenders, the great gateways and the staircases, the forecourts and outer provinces and the mountains in the background . . ." And yet Abrams, we are told, is haunted by a sense of futility. The more he studies, he tells the narrator, the more new information there is derived from the discoveries of archaeologists, the more difficult it is to make progress — a remark that not only recalls Penelope's weaving but reminds me, at least, of Erich Auerbach's statement describing his own attempt to reconstruct part of a lost culture: his observation, in the epilogue to his great book, that "if it had been possible for me to acquaint myself with all the work that has been done on so many subjects, I might have never reached the point of writing." Perhaps Auerbach was right after all about the virtues of blanks and opacity; perhaps too much knowing can lead to total inertia. And indeed, the narrator of *The Rings of Saturn* observes apropos of Abrams's model of the Temple that "it is difficult to see any change from one year to the next."

Abrams mournfully concludes his conversation by shar-
ing with the narrator his realization that that no amount
of reproduction can hope to capture the original:

> After all, if the Temple is to create the impression of
> being true to life, I have to make every one of the tiny
> coffers on the ceilings, every one of the hundreds of
> columns, and every single one of the many thousands
> of diminutive stone blocks by hand, and paint them
> as well. Now, as the edges of my field of vision are be-
> ginning to darken, I sometimes wonder if I will ever
> finish the Temple and whether all I have done so far
> has not been a wretched waste of time.

Sebald's model-maker is in fact based on a real person,
just as Proust's Saint-Loup was; in this case, the author's
friend Alec Garrard, who spent thirty years working on a
1:100 scale model of the Temple. But it is hard not to think
that if Garrard hadn't existed, Sebald would have had to
make him up. The unfinishable model of the Temple—a
structure that, as by now we know, has resisted accurate
representation throughout literary history—is the perfect
symbol of Sebald's manner as well as of his subject, both
of which are aligned with the pessimistic model of narrative, Erich Auerbach's "Hebrew" style, which derives its
uncanny power and devastating realism precisely from that
which cannot be represented. And why not? As we know,
sometimes it is safer to keep things in obscurity. It may
well be that the twisting history of the world is written
by the hiders—at least, the ones who hide successfully.

There is something else for which Sebald's story about

the doomed model-maker — the story that, for reasons that will be obvious by now, has a special hold over me — may be the ideal symbol. In *The Rings of Saturn,* Sebald describes Michael Hamburger as being simply "a writer," and yet the fact is that he was a distinguished poet and memoirist, too; and perhaps best known as a translator of German into English. Sebald's omission paradoxically draws attention to what he would elide. If the story about the model of the Temple may be taken as a metaphor for our tragic relationship to the past, for the inevitable failure of our attempts to preserve or rescue or re-create what is no longer present, the fraught elision of Hamburger's career as a translator gestures starkly to the "Hebrew" way with respect to literature in particular: to the futility of translation, indeed of any kind of writing that seeks to "carry across" (which is what the word "translate" means) an original into a new material, a new mode, a new time.

THE SUBJECT OF the difficulties of translation (to say nothing of a corollary subject, which is the heroism of anyone who attempts to translate) puts me in mind of a curious story that is set in Istanbul. Only there, as we know, could Auerbach write his paean to European literature, since Europe was destroying itself in precisely the manner that W. G. Sebald's novels can merely suggest without being able to describe. But there, too, another writer once labored, a Turk whose dream was to produce a perfect translation of a famous French text: François Fénelon's *Les aventures de Télémaque.*

By now we know about the enormous impact that

Fénelon's novel had on the mind of Europe, from the Enlightenment philosophers to Proust. But the appeal of the
French archbishop's ingenious expansion of Homer was
not limited to Europe or, indeed, to the West. Like Odysseus himself, you might say, *Les aventures de Télémaque*
"wandered greatly and knew the minds of many men." By
the first half of the nineteenth century there were translations into Turkish, Tatar, Bulgarian, Romanian, Arme-
nian, Albanian, Georgian, Kurdish, and Arabic, among
many other languages. In his 1855 memoir *La Turquie ac-
tuelle,* "Present-Day Turkey," the French writer and traveler
Jean-Henri-Abdolonyme Ubicini recalls that an attaché
to the Russian embassy once showed him a page from
an album on which the book's "famous opening lines"—
Calypso ne pouvait se consoler du départ d'Ulysse—had been
translated into "seventeen or eighteen languages." The
novel was one of the first Western works to achieve significant popularity east of the Hellespont, in the Middle
East, and even beyond. The name Tilîmâk, or Tilimak,
was known throughout the Levant; dramatizations of
Fénelon's novel for the theatrical and operatic stages were
performed in Beirut, Alexandria, and Istanbul.

It was particularly in the realm of the Ottoman sultan
that Fénelon's masterpiece found favor. No other work of
Western literature was as popular there during the nineteenth century. In his account of everyday life in the Istanbul neighborhood known as Pera (the Greek word for
"across," since this district lay across the Golden Horn
from the Old City), Ubicini observed that Fénelon was
one of only two French authors ordinary Turkish people

were likely to know, the other being Dumas. "They know Fénelon as the author of *Télémaque* and they know *Télémaque* as the first French book they ever held in their hands." He goes on to remark that his elderly landlady in Pera, an ordinary Ottoman citizen, had "learned by heart the most beautiful passages in the book." Most Turkish intellectuals owned a copy, sometimes the first edition; a course called *Télémaque* was even taught in the medical school. This is not as surprising as it may at first appear. Although the popular imagination has long cast the Ottoman Empire as impossibly mysterious and strange, an Eastern "other" as exotic in its way as Priam's Troy had been to the Greeks — opulent, decadent, corrupt, languid, and luxurious, the adjectives have remained the same for a hundred generations — a pro-Western turn was detectable as early as the early eighteenth century, during the so-called Tulip Era, when the Ottoman champions of modernizing reforms looked to Europe for new ideas as well as for the bulbs of the flowers with which they adorned their palaces. This eagerness to adapt to European tastes and import European goods led, in turn, to further reforms in the nineteenth century, and even more in the next, the twentieth, after Ataturk's revolution, when the secularized Turkish Republic provided such a warm welcome to European intellectuals fleeing oppression in the 1930s, giving rise to that joke by the Minister of Education. A certain literary tradition long established in the Ottoman Empire, to say nothing of much farther east, even as far as China, also helped to create the conditions for such a warm reception for *Les aventures:* the genre known as "Mirrors of Princes," educational treatises or tales intended for the political instruction or ethical edification of rulers.

And so Fénelon's adaptation of the *Odyssey* was able to flourish in the very land where, as Homer recounts, the wealthy and exotic Eastern city of Troy once flourished and where today the ruined remains of that lavish capital, finally reduced to rubble after ten years of siege as the result of the ruse of the Trojan Horse, that clever stratagem devised by Odysseus, are to be found near the modern town of Çanakkale, which was the first stop on the cruise my father and I took, the one that ultimately led to my moment of claustrophobic panic in Calypso's cave.

The best-known and most refined translation of *Les aventures de Télémaque* into Turkish was made in the late 1850s by no less a personage than the Grand Vizier of the Ottoman Empire: Yûsuf Kâmil Pasha, a distinguished statesman who served under the Sultan Abdülaziz. Kâmil Pasha's life had a Dickensian arc that seems like something out of a novel — one of those instances in which, as in the ring composition of which Erich Auerbach was so distrustful, the symmetries are so perfect that they strike us as artificial, even fictional. Born in Anatolia in 1808, Kâmil Pasha lost his father while still a small child, and therefore lacked the support enjoyed by so many provincial youths as they sought advancement through the elaborate maze of Ottoman politics. Nonetheless, after being taken under the wing of a well-connected uncle, he rose swiftly, first in Istanbul and then during a long posting to Egypt, by then a province of the Empire, where he married the daughter of the governor, Muhammad 'Ali Pasha. It was there, more to the point, that he began to study French, as did so many leading figures of the Ottoman intelligentsia throughout the nineteenth century, when a pervasive Francophilia coursed through the Empire like a fever. It was this love of all things French that led him to Fénelon. In a black-and-white photograph taken of Kâmil Pasha in old age, he wears a long tunic severely buttoned all the way to the throat, a garment that, to the Western eye, gives him an ecclesiastical air. The face is oval, the dark fez above it nicely balanced by the meticulously groomed white beard below; the nose at the center is large, hooked, confident. The eyes, beneath their dark angled brows, stare back at yours as if assessing you, at once inquisitive and patient: the eyes of someone who has managed to keep something back for himself at the table of the powerful.

Kâmil Pasha completed his translation in 1859 and published it in 1862. Himself a poet (sadly, many of his manuscripts were later destroyed in a devastating fire), he gave to his rendering of Fénelon's elegant French a remarkable literary polish: elaborate rhymes hidden in the prose, meticulous parallel constructions, a deft handling of the references to pagan gods and goddesses, which had to be adapted to suit the sensibilities of Muslim readers. This pressing need for sensitive adaptation of European texts to local tastes was, as it happens, one with which Erich Auerbach would become acquainted years later. Lecturing on Dante one day to his Turkish students, he felt compelled to omit a reference to the horrible punishment to which the Florentine poet condemns the prophet Mohammed, who, in the *Inferno,* appears in the ninth ditch of the Malebolge,

cleaved in half with his insides pouring out, such punishment, as barbaric as it seems to us now, being consonant
with medieval European attitudes toward the Muslim
peoples of the East, which no doubt contributed to the
long history of discord between them.

Kâmil Pasha's translation immediately won the admira-
tion of his peers. The Minister of Education appended a
foreword in which he alerted readers to the fact that although the text they were about to read seemed to be a
"story," it was in fact a book of *wisdom*. A second edition featured a laudatory preface by another minister who opined
with a touching optimism that, although literature consists
of a Babel of different tongues, meaning is universal, and a
unity exists beyond any cultural diversity — a principle that
seems to be demonstrated, if anything, by the fact that this
mid-nineteenth-century Muslim official's words so closely
echo Erich Auerbach's belief in *die gemeinsame Verbindung
der Kulturen,* the communal connectedness of cultures. Or
at least that was Auerbach's belief until he fled to Turkey,
at which point, in the words of one expert on his work, the
exiled scholar "drew a ring around his European self" and
retreated into it, having apparently soured on the idea of
connectedness, of there being hidden unities — a souring
that, I have no doubt, led to his endorsement, in the work
he would write during his Turkish exile, of the pessimistic
narrative style.

Kâmil Pasha died in 1876, at the age of sixty-eight.
A rich man by that time, thanks in part to the proceeds
of his translation of Fénelon, he had spent his final years
engaged in making admirable gestures of quiet generosity

that adhered to the high principles endorsed by Minerve in *Les aventures de Télémaque.* One of the beneficiaries of the philanthropies for which Yûsuf Kâmil Pasha became renowned was Istanbul University, into whose possession the large house he had shared with his wife eventually passed, following (since buildings as well as epic heroes can have multiple identities, as we know) stints first as a school and then as an orphanage — the latter being an incarnation that, we cannot help feeling, would have pleased Kâmil Pasha, given his early years as a fatherless boy: a nice circularity. In 1909, the great house, now part of the university, became a science building and then, after a devastating fire in which many of the original owner's books and papers were destroyed, was repurposed as the home of the literature faculty . . . This is as much as I was able to learn about the house of Fénelon's Turkish translator, struggling as I did over the course of some weeks to decipher Google translations of documents I'd found online, or relying on acquaintances in Istanbul to summarize articles or excerpts from books. But given that I am an optimist — or, as the last of the Holocaust survivors I interviewed put it, "sentimental" in my thinking about the past and the stories we tell about it — I cannot help believing that, despite the loss of so many books in the fire, the Grand Vizier's mansion was an ideal place for scholars to work, what with its fabulous views of the Sea of Marmara, shimmering like a mirage below, seeming to defy description: a difficulty that could well inspire someone to start wondering just how description works in the first place, how reality is mimicked in writing, how *die Wirklichkeit* becomes *dargestellte.*

This is where we will leave our stranger: staring out to sea, thinking no doubt of home — or at least, the home that he remembers. Let him sit there, at rest after his many peregrinations, exactly where chance or Fate (depending on how pessimistic or optimistic you are) left him in real life. He does not know, as we do, the history of the place he has come to; but then, he has ended up here after a long voyage, not only through space but, it is probably fair to say, through time: beginning with the sack of a great Anatolian city thirty-two centuries ago, then to the moment four hundred years later when the stories of the aftermath of that cataclysm begin to coalesce into a great poem, a poem so great that it is still being copied out many centuries in the future when, after another great Anatolian city is sacked, the copiers are scattered westward and the poem they keep copying so assiduously begins a new life in a new country; so great that two hundred years after that, after the sack of the city and the dispersal of the copiers, it inspires a wise and gentle priest of a religion Homer could not have conceived of to adapt and enhance this poem for the sake of a small child, a prince whose best potential self this new book is intended to mirror, although the prince's book will be read, over time, by many, many hundreds of thousands of ordinary people in distant places unimaginable to the gentle priest as he labored on his book, one of those places being Istanbul, the *City,* which is home to a sensitive and subtle Turk who, two centuries after the priest dies in exile, takes the book about the poem about the sack that took place a hundred generations earlier and from that book builds a house that, during yet another great cataclysm, becomes a sanctuary for literature and, finally, a home for our stranger.

No wonder he is tired.

So we will leave our wanderer there and not bother him with all this history, the vast chain of events that has brought him back to the coastline where all the myths began, because, as we know, obscurity has its uses, too: can be as solid and productive, as concrete and real, as illumination is. We do not want to distract him. Now it is time for this exile to set upon his great work, a book that will begin with an account of a technique that is as old as Homer, known as ring composition; a wandering technique that yet always finds its way home, a technique which, with its sunny Mediterranean assumption that there is indeed a connection between all things, the German Jew Erich Auerbach — no doubt forgivably just now, given the awful and twisted route that has brought him here, the dark road which yet, as he will one day finally admit, made his book possible — considers a little too good to be true.

ACKNOWLEDGMENTS

This book began its life as the 2019 Page-Barbour Lectures at the University of Virginia, an institution I am proud to call my alma mater and to which I was delighted to return for that signal honor. I am grateful to Chad Wellmon and James Loeffler, who originally extended the invitation to bring me home to Charlottesville, and to the many others who, over a hectic period of two years, did so much to arrange and organize my visit: particularly Martien Halvorson-Taylor, Laura Smith, and Creighton Coleman, all of them wonderful hosts. I am further indebted to the team at the University of Virginia Press for their warm support during the metamorphosis of the lectures into the book: Dick Holway, Ellen Satrom, Mary MacNeil, Helen Chandler, Jason Coleman, and my keen-eyed and wonderfully sympathetic copyeditor, Susan Murray.

Elif Batuman lent some crucial help with translation during the early stages of research for this project; I am, further, deeply indebted to a number of admirable works of scholarship on the reception of Fénelon and Auerbach in Turkey, particularly Serif Mardin's *The Genesis of Young Ottoman Thought* and Kader Konuk's *East West Mimesis*.

Every time I make a *nostos* to Charlottesville I am moved and overjoyed to be able to see once again the scholars who taught me when I was an undergraduate and the friends who have nurtured me ever since: Jenny Strauss Clay, Mary McKinley, Jon and Mary Mikalson, John and Mary Miller, Jahan Ramazani and Caroline Rody. Two people who were not part of that group, but into whose hands I later and happily fell, are the dedicatees of this book: great scholars and true humanists both, from whom I have learned very much indeed over the past twenty years, a rich period of friendship and (for me) apprenticeship that has made so much of my work possible.

Recent books from the
PAGE-BARBOUR AND RICHARD LECTURES